Re-bound 1998

Contents

5

Preface

The Hidden Epidemic

Scene: Dinner party

Guest: "I heard you're a writer. Are you writing anything now?"

Author: "Yes, a book about suicide among young people."

Guest: "Suicide! Did someone in your family commit suicide?"

Author: "No, why do you ask?"

Guest: "Why else would you be interested in a subject like that? It's so morbid."

Scene: Physician's office

Doctor: "Your checkup's fine. What are you working on these days?"

Author: "A book about young suicides."

Doctor: "How can you write a book about that? Those kids who try to kill themselves are all crazy!"

Scene: Parents' meeting at a primary school

A Mother: "I hear you are writing a book about teenage suicide. Who is it for?"

Author: "Oh, young people, parents, teachers, anybody."
Mother: "Don't you think some subjects are best left
untouched? Why put ideas into kids' heads?"

The subject of suicide is among the last of the taboo
topics in our society. Until recently people considered
sex and death the major taboo subjects, spoken of
only in whispers behind closed doors. But attitudes
have changed. Sexual taboos in speech as well as practice have all but vanished. And such once-forbidden
topics as homosexuality, bi-sexuality, rape, and abor-
tion are openly discussed. As for death as a subject, it
has become almost fashionable today. Books, television shows, and motion pictures dealing with some
aspects of death appear one after the other. And "than-
atology" societies that study death and help people
cope with it have grown up in many communities.

None of this is true of suicide. It is still a subject
cloaked in superstition, mystery, and sometimes ro-
manticism. And suicide among the young is the most
forbidden and repressed topic of all.

To adults, young people seem to have everything.
They are in the prime of life, filled with strength,
health, and the beauty of youth. "If only I were
young," thinks the fortyish father of a teenage boy, "I
could do so much with my life. I could be so happy."
And in his longing for a youth that has flown by, he
refuses to acknowledge that not all young people are
happy, that along with the excitement and growth of
the adolescent years there come pressures and fears
so strong in some that they far outweigh the joys of life.

Combined with many other factors, this nonrecogni-
tion by adults of the problems and concerns of the
young has been responsible for the alienation of young
people. And it has helped lead to their separation into
a culture in which drugs, alcohol, and violence have

come to be stubstitutes for love, feelings, and shared understandings. Suicide is one part of that culture, and it is the most disturbing and least comprehensible of all to adults.

"I think the reason that so many young people do commit suicide," explained a high school senior in a survey I conducted, "is because for so long older people did not realize that all of us kids *are not* having such a great time and that many of us have problems which are even worse than those our parents have. The reasons our problems are worse is because in most cases we are facing these things for the first time and we don't as yet know how to handle these situations. When parents see us in these states of depression, they figure we are just goofing off. And they add to the problems by reacting in such a way that it makes kids feel their parents don't care at all about what is bothering them."

Actually, most parents *do* care about what is bothering their children. But they prefer to play down the problems of the young, to think of them as insignificant, and assure themselves that their children will "grow out of them." Time after time, when a suicide has occurred a shocked parent will cry, "I don't understand it; he was such a happy kid." Or, "How could she? She had so much to live for."

It is a tragedy of our times that suicide among the young has become such a widespread problem that neither adults nor young people can continue to ignore it or to minimize the difficulties that lead up to it. The suicide rate among young people almost doubled in the 1970s compared with the 1960s, and studies show that it continues to rise, year after year. And while the actual rate of suicide among older people is higher than among the young, the rate of *increase* of young suicides far exceeds that of older groups. The sharply increased rates of young suicides, the numbers of young people involved in suicidal acts, and the numbers of families affected lead experts to speak of an "epidemic" of young suicides. <u>It is an epidemic that can be stopped only if the subject of suicide is brought out of <u>hiding</u> and faced openly and honestly.</u>

This book about adolescent suicide has been written for teenagers and young adults along with parents, teachers, and other concerned persons. I have tried throughout to present information and portray case histories without sensationalizing or romanticizing the material on the one hand or burdening the book with an overabundance of technicalities on the other. I do not believe that young people will be incited to suicidal behavior by learning about it, but I do firmly believe that they will continue to be prevented from helping others and themselves by being falsely "protected" from the subject.

Because suicide is such a taboo topic people have difficulty discussing it with candor. In an effort to gain insight into how young people regard the subject, I distributed a questionnaire to students at two private high schools in New York City and two colleges that are part of the New York State University system. The students were allowed to fill out the forms anonymously. I received 113 serious, carefully-thought-out responses that revealed the students' concern with the subject. A substantial majority had contact with others who had attempted suicide. A considerable number had made suicidal gestures and attempts themselves. Most also presented intelligent and well-reasoned answers to a question that related to the "right to suicide." Numerical results and excerpts from answers to the questions posed appear in appropriate places throughout the book.

During the preparation of the book I also spoke with young people who had made suicide attempts and with friends and family members whose lives had been touched by the suicidal acts of others, including the parents of several teenagers who had committed suicide. With their permission I taped many of their responses to my questions, and have included what they said in various chapters of the book, changing only names and other identifying details. I have also interviewed psychiatrists and public health workers who have treated suicidal young people or who have researched the broad areas of death and suicide. All the case histories in the book are based on real-life events, with changes made only to hide the identities of the people involved.

I'm grateful to the many people who helped as I prepared the book. Dr. Herbert Hendin shared his extensive knowledge about suicide with me, and generously allowed me to read relevant chapters of his book *The Age of Sensation* long before publication. Dr. Robert Jay Lifton graciously discussed his thoughts on the subject, and was especially helpful in offering his unique insights into the problems of the survivors of suicide. Dr. Joseph Cramer took time from his busy schedule to meet with me and help clarify my thinking about depression in young people. And Dr. Bruce L. Danto kindly sent me a chapter from his forthcoming book about violent sex and suicide, and made available his own research file on adolescent suicide.

Officials of the American Association of Suicidology, especially Charlotte P. Ross, were most helpful in answering a variety of questions and sending me their papers and articles. I'm indebted also to Emily Katz, Marilyn Katz, Loretta Lifton, and Joann Wasserman for distributing and collecting questionnaires; to my long-time colleague David C. Whitney for his invaluable editorial suggestions; to my Houghton Mifflin editor Mary K. Harmon for her never-failing support; and to my Pocket Books editor Pat MacDonald for

11

her dedication and the loving care she has given this book.

Finally, my husband, Dr. Samuel C. Klagsbrun, a "psychiatrist's psychiatrist," has been involved with this book from its inception, reviewing drafts and final versions of each chapter, and bringing to his comments his own sensitivity, his understanding of young people, and his enthusiasm for the project.

Francine Klagsbrun
New York City, 1976

Author's Note to Second Edition:

Since *Too Young To Die* first appeared, I've received scores of letters from young people and older ones, have been invited to speak to dozens of school groups, parents associations, and professional organizations, and have made numerous appearances on T.V. and radio panels. The concern about young suicides is real and deep, and youngsters as well as their parents and teachers hunger to speak openly about the fears and worries that press on them. A beginning has been made in breaking through the taboo and bringing the subject of youthful suicides into public consciousness. But the problem persists, and rising statistics continue to menace all those who are concerned about the young. The process of education and discussion must continue, and information about the issue must continue to be disseminated. Suicides among the young *can* be prevented. The first step is recognizing when a problem exists; the next is taking action to solve it.

All factual information has been updated for this new edition, and statistics are based on the latest available from the U.S. Public Health Service at the time the book was going to press. In addition, the list of addresses and phone numbers of Suicide Prevention and Crisis Intervention Centers in Appendix B has been totally revised. Every center listed has been personally contacted to be sure that it is actively involved in the work of suicide prevention. These centers serve as a lifeline to many troubled people, and I hope the new list will be of help to those in need.

Francine Klagsbrun
New York City, 1980

Part One: Realities

1 Myths and Realities

What Is True and What Is False?

"I was in the bathroom, and I took out the razor blades. About four other kids were banging on the door yelling, 'Hurry up! Hurry up! I have to go to the bathroom,' and I said, 'Yes, yes, I'll be out in a minute.'

"One of the girls barged in and saw me. I was all bloody, and there was blood all over the place. She ran and got my homeroom teacher, and she ran and got the director of the boarding school. They took me to the infirmary and bandaged me up. The nurse kept saying, 'You know, you just missed your artery; you could have died.' I just looked at the lady, wondering what it was she thought I had been trying to do. Crazy.

"Then they took me to the director's office and called my doctor. After that they let me go back to my room for a minute to get my nightgown and cigarettes, and then they smuggled me back to the infirmary. I wasn't allowed to tell anyone where I was going. The director kept saying, 'There's nothing wrong, girls, nothing to worry about.' None of my roommates knew what had happened. I wanted to speak to some of my friends, but the director wouldn't let me.

"Next morning they woke me, and my parents were there. I couldn't believe my folks were there. I wouldn't talk to them. I yelled, 'Go away, go away,' and turned over and tried to go back to sleep. The school had made it clear that I would be expelled, and my parents wanted to take me right home. But I insisted on saying goodbye to some of my friends. They let me speak to a few, maybe three. And then I left. They smuggled me out of there. They didn't give a damn about me. I guess they thought it would be better for the school if I didn't see anybody. All they cared about was running a normal school day."

Laurie K. is sixteen years old. In this excerpt from a taped interview, she described her second suicide attempt in a year. Laurie discussed the event with an interviewer calmly, showing little emotion. But when asked to tell how she felt as she slashed her wrists, she snapped, "Oh, no, that's not for publication. That's too personal."

To Laurie, the desperate suicide act and the feelings that drove her to it seem unique and terribly personal. She would have difficulty imagining that someone else could feel as sad, as lonely, and as rejected as she. But Laurie does not have a unique story. Thousands of teenagers have made similar attempts on their lives. And they, like Laurie, have been "smuggled" away from classmates and friends, their deed hidden deep in the dark closet of social disgrace.

Suicide, and especially suicide among the young, frightens people, and it threatens them. The self-destructive act of a single person questions the basis of everyone's existence, the very meaning of life itself. How much easier it is to hide suicides and suicide attempts, to ignore them or deny them, than to cope with the unspoken questions they raise. How much easier to accept half-truths and pat explanations than to delve into the causes and motives behind a young person's wish to die.

Over the years many myths have grown about suicide. Some myths allow people to fool themselves, just as the administrators of Laurie's school fooled themselves into thinking that by keeping Laurie "under wraps" they could hide her suicide attempt. Other myths help push away the uneasiness the idea of suicide arouses, and substitute for it a complacent "it can't happen here" feeling.

Test yourself. Would you say the following statements are true or false?

1. Debbie P. threatens to kill herself whenever she feels hurt or angry. "You'll be sorry when I'm dead!" is one of her favorite endings to arguments with her parents. Because Debbie talks so much about suicide, she won't actually attempt it.

2. Burt N. tried to kill himself by taking an overdose of sleeping pills. His parents found him and rushed him to the hospital, where doctors pumped his stomach. After the pain and fright he experienced, Burt probably will not attempt suicide again.

3. Emily G. had been depressed for some time. She told her closest friend that she has nothing to live for, and wants to die. During the past few days, however, Emily has acted relaxed and cheerful. We can safely assume that her suicidal thoughts have now passed.

You should have answered *false* to each of the statements. Most people would not have, because the myths these statements represent are so widely held that few people know the more disturbing truths about suicide.

For example, one of the most accepted fallacies about suicide is that people like Debbie P. who talk about killing themselves never do. Such a misbelief allows the listener to ignore the talk and avoid taking action. Psychiatrists and psychologists who specialize

19

in treating teenagers agree that those who threaten suicide often have serious suicidal thoughts. Their threats and talk serve as clues that they need help. When others ignore the clues many do go on to kill themselves.

Parents and friends of a boy like Burt N. might find comfort in believing that the shame and pain of a suicide attempt will prevent the attempter from trying again. The reverse is true, however. For a suicide attempter, the first time is the hardest. Having once crossed the barrier from thinking to acting, the person finds it easier to try a second or third time if the conditions that brought about the attempt have not improved. Research has shown that of every five people who complete suicide, four have made one or more previous attempts.

It would be reassuring to know that someone like Emily G., who seems improved after being depressed, no longer feels suicidal. The fact is that a large number of suicides among depressed persons take place just at the time when the person begins to feel well. A depressed person may appear relaxed because he or she has come to a final decision about committing suicide, or simply has more energy at this time to carry out the act. The period immediately after a depression can be the most dangerous time of all, a time for friends and family to be constantly on their guard.

People hold many other misleading ideas about suicide. Most of the wrong things they say grew out of old superstitions and myths that have been repeated over the years. Here are some common fallacies you might hear:

"Anyone who tries to kill himself has got to be crazy."

In reality, most suicidal people cannot be labeled "psychotic" or "insane." Although people who try to

20

kill themselves usually feel deeply despairing and hopeless, they do not necessarily suffer from severe mental illness.

"Nothing could have stopped her once she decided to kill herself."

This is wrong on several counts. Even the most severely suicidal person has mixed feelings about death, wavering until the very last moment between wanting to live and wanting to die. Suicidal persons send out many clues and messages that might allow others to save them—if the others are listening. In addition, no one is suicidal all the time. Sometimes death wishes may be overpowering, but at other times the person tries to cope with life. Many suicides can be prevented.

"I'll bet he was rich. Those rich kids kill themselves because they're bored with life."

Another misconception. Statistics show that suicide strikes equally among rich and poor adults and young people.

"It's not surprising. Suicide runs in her family, you know."

The truth is, suicidal tendencies cannot be inherited. For various psychological reasons, one suicide in a family may lead to others. But, biologically, suicides do not "run in families."

"He killed himself on that gloomy Wednesday. The weather must have oppressed him."

In fact, oppressive weather has little to do with causing suicide. Studies have shown that suicide rates go up during the spring months, reaching a peak in April and May, and down during winter months, with low points in December and January. Perhaps the sense of rebirth and joy that abounds at springtime makes de-

21

pressed people more aware of their own inner gloom and despondency. The belief that dull, dismal weather causes suicide probably goes back to a superstitious view of suicide as a dark and mysterious act.

"Better stay with her at night because that's when suicides usually happen."

Wrong again. More suicides occur between 3:00 and 6:00 in the evening—presumably when the suicidal person can be seen and stopped—than late at night when others would be asleep. The mistaken notion that most suicides occur in the dark of night stems too from a superstition about the blackness of the deed.

"Don't mention suicide in front of her. It'll give her ideas."

Another common mistake. You don't give a suicidal person morbid ideas by speaking about suicide. The person has the ideas. You can help by bringing suicidal thoughts into the open so they can be talked about.

"It couldn't have been suicide. He didn't leave a note."

Mystery stories and movies to the contrary, only a small percentage—about 15 percent—of people who kill themselves leave suicide notes. The mistaken idea that all suicides leave notes has led authorities to mislabel many suicidal deaths without notes as accidents.

"Oh, there was something romantic about their suicide. They loved each other so much they wanted to die together."

The myth of romantic suicide is probably the most insidious and destructive of all. Romanticizing suicide places it in the realm of artistry and beauty, and removes it from the grim realities of everyday life. It is much easier to sympathize with the sweet sorrows of Romeo and Juliet than to acknowledge the real-life suffering endured by parents of a young couple who shared a suicide pact. It is infinitely more comforting to praise the moving poems of the young suicide Sylvia Plath than to contemplate the heights she might have achieved had she lived. Real-life suicide is neither romantic nor beautiful. For young people it represents life unfulfilled—a tragic end to years of unhappiness and misunderstanding.

The myths build, one on another, accepted as truths by most people. And the facts, the appalling facts and figures about young suicides, remain unknown.

How many people know that suicide kills far more teenagers and young adults than do such dread diseases as cancer and heart ailments? Each year more than 5,000 young people between the ages of fifteen and twenty-four die as suicides. Only accidents claim more young lives. And the ratio of suicide to other causes of death may be much higher than now known because many suicides are hidden by families and reported as accidents or even murders.

How many people know that the suicide rate among young people in the 1970s was almost three times higher than it had been in the 1950s? It was almost twice as high as it had been in the 1960s. (Suicide rates are calculated on the basis of the number of suicides per 100,000 persons in any age group.) In 1957 the suicide rate for men and women between the ages of fifteen and twenty-four was 4.0 suicides per 100,000. In 1967 it rose to 7.0. It jumped to 13.6 in 1977, an increase of more than 300 percent in twenty years! The rate among males in this age group leaped from 6.4 in 1957 to an alarming 21.8 in 1977. The rate among females, always much lower than that of males, still more than doubled—from 1.8 in 1957 to 5.3 in 1977. (For suicide rates among young people from 1956 to 1977, broken down by age and sex, see Appendix A.)

Suicide attempt rates, too, have risen dramatically. We know less about the numbers of suicide attempts made each year because most attempts are not reported to official agencies. Some experts estimate, however, that for every young person who completes suicide, there may be fifty to a hundred others who attempt it. That means that there may be 300,000 to 500,000 young people like Laurie K. in the United States who attempt to end their lives each year. And while there are few suicides *recorded* among children under fourteen years old—medical examiners almost always list questionable deaths at these ages as accidents—hospitals have treated many eight- and ten-year-old suicide attempters. From all indications, their numbers too are growing rapidly.

One clue to the numbers of teenagers and young adults whose lives have been touched by suicide and suicide attempts comes from this author's survey. Of the students in high schools and colleges who responded to the author's questionnaire about suicide, more than one in ten said they themselves had attempted suicide. Other students wrote in that they had seriously contemplated suicide although they had not acted on those thoughts. More than half the students (58 percent) reported that they knew people who had attempted suicide. Nearly a third (29 percent) said they had friends or relatives who actually had killed themselves.

Clearly, suicide intrudes on the lives of many young people. Much remains unknown about suicide among the young. But the myths and mysteries that have grown up around the subject blur the knowledge we do have, and prevent people from coping intelligently with a problem that grows more pressing each year.

2 Motives and Messages

‖‖⊏∋‖‖‖‖‖‖‖‖⊏∋‖‖‖‖‖‖‖⊏∋‖‖‖‖‖‖‖⊏∋‖‖‖‖‖‖‖⊏∋‖‖‖‖‖‖‖⊏∋‖‖‖‖‖‖‖⊏∋‖‖‖‖‖‖‖⊏∋‖‖‖‖‖‖‖⊏∋‖‖‖

Suicide As Communication

Jules B. was fourteen years old when he attempted suicide. Impulsively, and with little apparent warning, Jules opened his bedroom window, yelled, "I'm going to jump," and began to step out. His father dashed in from another room, grabbing the boy from behind. The two wrestled on the floor, with Jules kicking, biting, and screaming until his father pinned him down.

On the surface, Jules appeared to have taken the awesome step of trying to kill himself because of a trivial matter. A camera buff, the boy had longed for a Polaroid SX 70, which develops pictures in seconds. When his parents refused to buy the expensive camera, he shouted and cried, then threatened to kill himself. The tantrums left Jules's father even more adamant than before in his refusal. But his mother wavered, then finally agreed that she would buy the camera for Jules's next birthday if he achieved an A average in school. Jules seemed to accept his mother's conditions. He acted calm and cheerful that evening as he showed a friend his photographic equipment. Then suddenly he stood at the window sill, shouting his suicidal threat.

25

At sessions with a therapist afterward, Jules spoke of wanting to die in order to punish his parents. "I want them to be sorry," he said, "really sorry for all the rotten things they've done to me."

Over the course of several months, during which Jules and his parents met regularly with the therapist, they began to gain the first insights they had ever had into their relationships. Jules's parents came to see how their actions had led their son to feelings of depression and hopelessness. At the same time, they came to recognize, as did Jules, that the boy's own temperament, personality, and extreme sensitivity made him especially responsive to their moods and attitudes toward him. Another child in a similar situation may not have felt pushed to quite the extreme Jules reached.

The complex relationships in Jules's family characterize many other families. Parents almost always blame themselves and receive the blame of others when suicidal acts occur in their families. While there is no doubt that the ways in which parents treat their children have a crucial influence on the children, a child's own nature plays a vital part, too, in determining how she or he will react to family pressures.

Jules, an only child, had been idolized by his mother from the time of his birth. She indulged him and pampered him, and deluged friends with tales of his exploits. Jealous and resentful of his wife's total devotion to the child, Jules's father found every opportunity to cut the boy down. As time went on his attitude toward Jules became increasingly bitter and harsh, and he meted out severe punishment for even the slightest misbehavior.

Highly intelligent and sensitive, Jules grew up feeling confused about himself and the world around him. Was he exceptionally good or exceptionally bad? Did he deserve glowing praise or degrading punishment?

The answers depended on which parent's view he took. Adding to the boy's confusion were constant arguments between his parents, who came to disagree over almost every area of their life together. Time and again Jules found himself caught in the middle, called upon by both parents to take a side in their quarrels and to pass judgment on their actions.

Jules learned early in life how to manipulate his parents. With cuteness and boyish charm he became adept at playing off one parent against the other. And when cuteness and charm failed, Jules turned to angry demands and temper tantrums.

As Jules reached adolescence the bitterness between his parents grew more intense, and the boy's own confusion, anger, and despair increased. He began to withdraw from family and friends and to immerse himself in hobbies that kept him isolated and secluded. His appearance became shabby, and days would go by in which he neither showered nor changed his clothes. In spite of his very high IQ score of 140, he could barely keep up with his schoolwork, using the classroom as a platform for angry outbursts and disruptive behavior. Jules became such a problem that one school principal expelled him and a second quickly placed him on probation.

The situation continued to deteriorate. Jules made more outrageous and insistent demands on his parents, and they reacted in contradictory and inconsistent ways. True to their pattern, when Jules demanded the Polaroid camera, his father angrily refused and his mother gave in—but only after establishing conditions that, in his state of mind, Jules would find impossible to meet. The incident, a "last straw" for Jules, led to the suicidal outburst that came close to disaster.

Many inner motives and drives worked together to push Jules toward a suicide attempt. On one level, Jules's actions continued his old technique of alternately manipulating and bullying his parents. "I'm going to kill myself," he threatened as a way to intimidate them, and when they ignored the threat, he became determined to get even with them. "They'll be sorry when I'm dead," he thought to himself, replaying the fantasy of every child who has been hurt, angered, or rejected. Beneath such thinking lay a kind of magical belief that somehow after death he, Jules, would still be present to get satisfaction from his parents' suffering.

On another level, death—real death—represented an escape for Jules, the only way out of a situation that he viewed as intolerable. Deep within him Jules felt confused and hopelessly trapped into a pattern of life he could not control. At the moment he stepped toward the window, the tensions and pain that had been building for years could no longer be contained. A part of Jules truly wanted to die, to find relief from his misery.

And then, perhaps most important, Jules's suicide attempt became a means of affecting his parents in a way he could never reach them before. For Jules, as for a large number of suicidal persons, the act of suicide served as a last, desperate attempt to communicate his unhappiness. It became a way of saying, "Look at me! Help me! I can't go on!" While trying to die Jules pleaded silently, "Listen to me so that I may live." While taking revenge on his parents he cried, "Love me so that I don't need to hate you."

The complicated mixture of feelings and motives involved in Jules's suicide attempt typifies most suicides and attempted suicides. Almost all share the confused pull between loving and hating; between feeling hopeless yet wishing for a last-minute solution to their problems; between wanting to break away from family and friends while wanting desperately, pathetically, to communicate with them.

These contradictory feelings come through again and again in the suicide notes left by people who have killed themselves. One study of suicide notes showed how a series of rationalizations allowed people to move from thinking about suicide to attempting it. For the study, sociologist Jerry Jacobs analyzed 112 suicide notes written by teenagers and adults. Through the notes he traced the thought processes of the writers. In a large proportion of cases the suicides had found themselves faced with a pressing and intolerable problem that added to the many unhappy situations they had previously suffered. Convinced that they had not created the problem themselves and that they themselves could not solve it, they also believed themselves incapable of making others understand how hopeless they felt. Finally, each concluded reluctantly that death represented the only way out.

"Believe me I tried to cope with my problems but I couldn't," a seventeen-year-old boy summed up his situation.

"I know this won't seem the right thing to you but from where I stand it seems like the best solution," a teenage girl explained.

"There is nothing I could say that would make you see what was happening to me. I am sorry," a college student wrote to his father.

And underlying all the explanations, the apologies, and the accusations of the suicide notes one message came through, unspoken yet clearly there: "Had someone helped me I would not have had to do this."

Another study pointed up the way suicidal people relate to others at the final moments before death. For this study two psychologists, Edwin S. Shneidman and Norman L. Farberow, asked a carefully selected group of people to compose suicide notes as though they were about to kill themselves. Using computers and various psychological tests, the psychologists then compared the contents and vocabulary of these fake notes with those of real suicide notes taken from the Los Angeles County coroner. They found that the genuine notes included more angry feelings and more wishes for revenge than the fake notes. The genuine notes also gave more concrete instructions to survivors and used more specific names of people, places, and things. For the suicidal, these notes—and the act itself—served as a means of reaching out to specific people, of influencing them and controlling them even after death.

In other studies of suicide the same psychologists, Shneidman and Farberow, coined the term "cry for help" to describe many suicidal acts. Sometimes consciously, more often unconsciously, the suicidal person uses an attempt at self-destruction as a plea to be noticed and helped. Usually this desperate cry for help comes only after quieter calls and less dramatic messages have brought no results. Almost always suicidal people aim their actions at specific family members or friends, the key people in their lives whom experts on suicide call "significant others."

Shneidman and Farberow popularized the term "cry for help" mostly in regard to suicide attempts, where help can still prevent tragedy. But the same concept of a cry, of a message being sent and an impact being made, often can extend to the death act itself. In many situations suicide becomes a way of communicating with others after all other forms of communication have broken down.

"Even the despairing suicide of a young person is in a sense, from his perspective, a search for affirmation," explains psychiatrist Robert Jay Lifton, who has written a great deal about attitudes toward death. "That person tries to say through suicide, 'this is unsatisfactory and by implication there must be some better alternative that I cannot find in my life, but that I want to affirm or at least make known by killing myself.' "

Obviously, differences exist between the motives and methods of young people who attempt suicide and those who actually kill themselves. Many persons who make suicide attempts have no intention of dying. They act out their cry for help consciously, and they choose methods that give them the greatest leeway to be saved. They may take a small dosage of pills that could be barely lethal. They may turn on the gas in a closed room, but leave a leak in a wall or window unplugged. Or they may make superficial slashes on their wrists. Young men and women more determined to die usually use more violent and destructive methods.

Most teenage boys and young men who kill themselves do so with guns and explosives. Hanging themselves is the second most common method, and taking pills and poisons is the third. Girls and young women who kill themselves do so most often with pills and poisons, but guns and explosives come as a very close second. Hanging is the third most common method of suicide among girls. On the other hand, boys and girls who have attempted suicide without fatal results generally have not used such violent methods as guns and hanging. Most have taken pills or poisons, or slashed their wrists with razor blades—all methods that allow time for rescue.

Yet for all the differences, parents, friends, and even professionals who overemphasize distinctions between the motives of young suicide attempters and those who complete suicide play a dangerous game. Often only a thin line separates the two, and many an attempter who may have "just wanted attention" ends as a grim suicide statistic.

In too many cases fate or chance rather than intention determines who will live and who will die. Sometimes persons bent on self-destruction, who use the most lethal methods possible, survive almost miraculously. People have shot themselves through the heart and

31

survived. They have jumped from enormous heights or hung themselves from binding nooses and survived. Others, who seemed less determined to die, did so almost accidentally.

The poet Sylvia Plath is an example of a tragic death that probably resulted accidentally from a suicide attempt. Plath had made several attempts before her final one. This time, as at others, she set the stage for rescue. Earlier, she had hired a young woman to help her care for her children. With the knowledge that the woman was to arrive at a specified time, Plath sealed her kitchen and turned on the gas, after first leaving a note about how to reach her doctor. When the woman arrived, however, she found the building locked. She could not enter, nor could she awaken Plath's neighbor, who had been knocked unconscious by the escaping gas. By the time workmen forced her door open, Sylvia Plath was dead. "She gambled for the last time, having worked out that the odds were in her favor . . . ," wrote A. Alvarez, who described her death in his book *The Savage God*. "Her calculations went wrong and she lost."

On the other side of the coin, even the most self-destructive person, who sees death as the only way out, is torn between wanting to live and wanting to die. One young woman who had made up her mind to kill herself spent weeks planning every detail of her suicide. Satisfied that nothing could stop her from death, she leapt seven stories from her apartment window. By a twist of fate, a tree broke her fall and she survived. Later she described how she felt as she jumped from the building: "As I began to fall," she said, "I wanted more than anything to be able to turn back, grab hold of the window ledge and pull myself up."

The possibilities of unintentional deaths and the ambivalent feelings most suicidal persons share emphasize the potential for death in almost every suicide attempt and the unanswered appeal to life in almost every completed suicide. (The exceptions are those people whose suicidal acts result from such severe mental illness that the person loses touch with reality, and behaves in irrational and bizarre ways.)

You can think of the steps toward suicide in many cases as taking place along a continuum. Picture a teenage boy, for example, who has come to feel miserable and trapped by the life he leads. For a variety of reasons he believes he cannot make others—especially his parents—understand his feelings. Maybe lines of communication among family members have never been open. Or maybe he is so sensitive and isolated he has no perspective on his situation. Rather than try to talk to others, he pulls further and further into himself. Or he begins to drink heavily or take drugs or act violently and disruptively.

One day after an argument with his father the young man makes a suicide attempt that temporarily brings his parents rushing to his side. The attempt is a weak one, however, and is soon put out of mind by parents and friends. A few months later the boy makes a more serious suicide attempt, a more agonized appeal for help. This too arouses some reaction, but brings little improvement to his life. His final, fatal suicidal act then becomes his ultimate message: "Only my death can convey the misery of my life."

The case of Jules B., described in the opening of this chapter, illustrates just such a progression. Jules moved from point to point in escalating his signs of despair, but could bring about no loosening of his family's hold on him. He failed in his schoolwork. He had temper tantrums. He withdrew from family and friends, and became slovenly and sullen. Finally he stood at the edge of his bedroom window and at that point his life began to change.

Marion H. had to go much further before being

33

heard. On several occasions after arguments with her parents or after deep disappointments she slashed her wrists superficially. Each time she appeared afterward at breakfast or dinner wearing short-sleeved tops that clearly revealed her bandaged wrists. Nobody in her family noticed. Nobody paid attention either to her growing depression and silent withdrawals until the day she had to be rushed to the hospital, with her artery cut, bleeding almost to death.

Until the last moment before a suicide attempt, suicidal people give out messages and clues: some by the way they act, others by the things they say. "I wish I were dead," a depressed young woman might say. Or, "I want to kill myself," she might whine in a self-pitying way that annoys her friends. But behind her self-involvement lies a plea for someone to stop her. Less openly, a college student might begin giving his possessions to his friends, mumbling simply, "I won't need these anymore." A boy might ask his teacher, "How can a person arrange to leave his body to a medical school?" or "How many aspirin would someone have to take to kill himself?"

In a thousand different ways potential suicides call out to those who might help them. If others learn to recognize the messages and act on the clues, they often can prevent the final, irrevocable message, the one that says, "I gave up."

3 The Sad and the Lonely

Recognizing Clinical Depression

He always wanted to explain things.
But no one cared.
So he drew.
Sometimes he would draw,
and it wasn't anything.
He wanted to carve it in stone
or write it in the sky,
and it would be only him and the sky and
the things inside him that needed saying.
It was after that he drew the picture.
It was a beautiful picture.
He kept it under his pillow
and would let no one see it.
He would look at it every night
and think about it.
When it was dark and his eyes were closed,
he could still see it.
When he started school,
he brought it with him,
not to show anyone,
just to have along like a friend.

It was funny about school.
He sat at a square, brown desk,
like all the other square, brown desks.
He thought it should be red.
And his room was a square, brown room,
like all the other rooms.
It was tight and close and stiff.
He hated to hold the pencil and chalk,
his arms stiff, his feet flat on the floor.
stiff,
the teacher watching and watching.
The teacher came and spoke to him.
She told him to wear a tie
like all the other boys.
He said he didn't like them.
She said it didn't matter!
After that, they drew.
He drew all yellow.
It was the way he felt about morning,
and it was beautiful.
The teacher came and smiled at him.
"What's this?" she said, "Why don't you
draw something like Ken's drawing?
Isn't that beautiful?"
After that, his mother bought him a tie,
and he always drew airplanes and rocketships
like everyone else.
And he threw the old picture away.
And when he lay alone looking at the sky,
it was big and blue and all of everything,
but he wasn't anymore.
He was square inside and brown,
and his hands were stiff.
He was like everyone else.
The things inside that needed saying
didn't need it anymore.
It had stopped pushing.

It was crushed.
Stiff.
Like everything else.

—written by a high school senior
two weeks before killing himself

Simply and movingly, the boy who wrote this poem described the closed tight world of the severely depressed. A sensitive and artistic child, he had been made to conform to a rigid system, and he could not accept the conformity. But beyond that, for deeper reasons the poem does not reveal, he became overwhelmed by his situation, numbed and deadened to all of life. Like him, other depressed people come to feel "stiff" and "crushed" by the burdens of their lives. Lonely, engulfed by sadness, they do not know how to reach out to others, to find relief from the anxieties that plague them. And when the depression itself becomes insufferable, some begin to see death as their only way out, their escape from the "square, brown" room of their universe.

The majority of people who commit suicide do so as a result of the kind of devastating depression the poet experienced. That does not mean that every depressed person commits, attempts, or even thinks about suicide, nor that every suicide comes about as a result of depression. But a large number of suicides and suicide attempts among young people and older ones can be linked in some ways to a state of severe depression.

Everybody gets depressed from time to time. A boy who had been a top student in high school is rejected by his first-choice college. He feels angry and hurt, shamed and suddenly inadequate. He refuses for a few days to see his friends or to speak to anyone. A woman doesn't receive a job promotion she sought. She finds herself snapping at co-workers and having great difficulty concentrating on the job she does have.

37

A family moves with much excitement to a new location. Once settled, however, the children become listless and homesick for their old friends; the parents act irritable and dejected.

Feeling low or sad or blue is a normal reaction to the stresses and strains of everyday life, as normal and appropriate as feeling happy or hopeful. For most people, a depressed mood may last a few hours, a few days, or even a few weeks. It comes as part of life, but it doesn't totally disrupt life.

The moods of depression most people experience barely scratch the surface of the deep, despairing depression that physicians call clinical depression. Clinical depression may involve many of the same feelings as ordinary depression, but the feelings are far deeper and more destructive, encompassing the totality of the person's thoughts and actions.

"There is such a terrible nothingness," explained a woman who had suffered from clinical depression. "There is no beauty; there's no love. There's no hope, no joy. And the only thing there is is that terrible fear and an awful desire to die . . . It's hell when you don't have to die to go to hell. All you have to do is be depressed."

Profound feelings of worthlessness and lack of self-esteem lie at the base of many severe depressions, according to psychiatrists, and these feelings separate clinical depression from ordinary sadness and grief. Back in the early 1900s, Sigmund Freud contrasted clinical depression with the emotions people have when mourning a death. A severely depressed person, like a grief-stricken mourner, experiences "painful dejection, cessation of interest in the outside world," and other forms of deep unhappiness, Freud explained in a famous paper called "Mourning and Melancholia." But in addition, depressed people tend to blame themselves for whatever bad things have happened to them,

nd they punish themselves, again and again, for the
ailings they believe they have.

Along the same lines, in a definitive book about
lepression written many years later, Aaron T. Beck
lescribed three major characteristics of deeply depressed people.

First, depressed people have a negative view of
themselves, said Dr. Beck. They constantly "put themselves down" and believe themselves helpless to
change their lives. A beautiful teenage girl who developed a mild case of acne, for example, blamed
herself for eating chocolate, decided she was ugly and
repulsive now, and refused to go out with friends.

Second, depressed people have a negative view of
the world and their relation to it. They distort reality
so that even the slightest challenge becomes overwhelming. In one case, a depressed high school student who had always received A's in his coursework
received a B in one course. On the basis of that one
grade the student decided not to apply to college because, even if accepted, he would not be able to keep
up with his classmates.

Finally, depressed people have a negative view of
the future. They expect little good to come their way.
And, as their depression deepens, they give up hope
that they will ever feel better. "The worst is that you
absolutely know things will never change and you're
never going to get well," said a woman who had, in
fact, recovered from severe depression.

The helpless and hopeless feelings clinically depressed people have show themselves in their actions.
Depressed people may have trouble sleeping, and
keep awakening in the middle of the night or the early
morning hours. Or, just the opposite, they may sleep
all the time, dozing constantly in the middle of the

day or the early evening. They usually lose their appetites, eat little, and become drawn and gaunt.

People who feel deeply depressed want to be alone much of the time. They withdraw from family and friends, keeping silently to themselves. They lose their sense of humor, and may cry for the most trivial reasons. Or, when the depression becomes especially severe, they find themselves incapable of crying even when they want to. To people suffering from clinical depression any kind of decision becomes difficult, and even the slightest task seems insurmountable. The depressed move slowly, slowly, as though every step and every gesture takes enormous effort.

Any one of the symptoms of clinical depression, taken alone, could be accepted as a normal reaction to a pressing problem or to a sad event. One way you can recognize that a situation is severe and potentially dangerous is by noticing a cluster of symptoms—sleeplessness plus loss of appetite plus loneliness and withdrawal from others. Another clue to the severity of a depression is the length of time it lasts. A person who acts sad and dejected for a few days or who doesn't sleep for a few nights is probably not headed for clinical depression. But a person whose anxiety and unhappiness go on relentlessly, week after week, probably feels stifled by fear and hopelessness.

Through the things they say and the things they do, clinically depressed people cry out for help. Their silence and their complaints, their helplessness and hopelessness are clues to the depths of their despair. For such people bland assurances that "everything will be all right" or simplistic advice to "take it easy" are useless. The clinically depressed need real help. And the help must come in the form of care and understanding by family and friends, and, in many situations, professional treatment by a trained psychiatrist, psychologist, social worker, or physician sensitive to the problems of depression.

Depressed people whose symptoms go unnoticed or unattended may pull further into themselves. For many, as the depression deepens, images of death begin to take hold. Suicide becomes a real alternative to a life of misery. Some become obsessed with suicidal thoughts, planning their deaths with the utmost care. "We talked of death, and this was life to us," wrote Anne Sexton in a memoir of her friend Sylvia Plath. These two brilliant young poets spent hours together reviewing every detail of their suicide attempts. And in the end both killed themselves.

Even after outward symptoms of depression disappear, suicidal thoughts and wishes may continue. Sometimes the person appears happy because inwardly he or she has made a resolute decision to commit suicide, and no longer feels tortured by indecision. And sometimes, with the draining depression gone, the person can muster sufficient energy to carry out long-dreamed-of plans for death. This spurt of energy and activity immediately after a depression can lead directly to suicide. Time and again physicians warn friends and relatives of someone who has been seriously depressed to stay especially alert for hints and concealed suicide threats the person might drop. And the alert should last for at least six months after the depression has lifted.

The classical symptoms of clinical depression—withdrawal, crying, inability to sleep, and so on—do not make up the complete picture of depression among teenagers and younger children. Among them, symptoms of depression may be more concealed, more misleading, and more often misinterpreted. For these reasons, many psychiatrists speak of depression among the young as a "masked depression" in which true feelings have become camouflaged.

41

Young people tend to act out their feelings rather than talk about them, to be impatient and impulsive rather than cautious and thoughtful about what they say and do. As a result, teenagers faced with an agonizing problem or suffering from an intolerable situation may not show the slow-moving, oppressive symptoms of despair common among older people. Instead they cover their feelings with actions—quick, impulsive, sometimes irrational actions that leave them no time to ponder their unhappiness.

A teenager who becomes seriously depressed may suddenly switch from being a pleasant, well-behaved student to a wild and unruly one. Another may drop out of school altogether, or when the going gets especially rough, run away from home. Other young people show their depression by acting bored and listless and unable to concentrate on even the simplest tasks. Someone who had received top grades may begin flunking courses. Someone who had been a healthy athlete may suddenly develop physical aches and pains that have no physiological basis.

Typical of a masked depression is the case of sixteen-year-old Mary T. Shortly after her parents had agreed to a divorce, Mary developed severe pains in her legs and back. Each morning she complained so bitterly of her unbearable pain that her mother allowed her to stay home from school, and in bed a good part of the time. Days and then weeks went by and the girl refused to budge from her bed. Neither Mary's physician nor a series of consultants called in could uncover anything physically wrong with her. And yet she moaned of her agonizing pain.

After months of following the routine of a bedridden invalid, Mary agreed to meet with a psychiatrist. During one of her sessions, as she spoke of her life at home, Mary broke down into bitter tears and began to pour out her unhappiness. She loved her father dearly, and missed him dreadfully now that he had moved out of her house. But because she believed her father had hurt her mother she felt torn with guilt about her strong attachment to him. Rather than anger her mother by revealing her love for her father, she kept all her feelings bottled up tight within her. Her body literally hurt from her deep emotional pain, and she wanted nothing more than to stay in bed and nurture her sadness.

Wayne O., a fifteen-year-old, showed different masked symptoms of depression. Wayne disappeared from home one day, leaving no clues to his whereabouts. His frantic parents tried every lead they could, but finally had to call in the police. Two police officers managed to find the boy and bring him home. Once there, he refused to discuss the incident with his parents or anyone else. When asked about it, he answered noncommittally, "I was stupid to run away; I shouldn't have done it."

About a year later Wayne made a serious suicide attempt. Under psychiatric care at a hospital, he began to speak about the conflicts and frustrations of his life. Wayne had grown up as the youngest of six children, with an eight-year age span between him and the next youngest child. By the time Wayne reached his teen years all his brothers and sisters had moved away from home, most of them to different cities and states. Wayne's parents had never paid much attention to him, but now he found them more distant than ever. With a growing sense of fear and helplessness, he watched them drink themselves into a state of violent drunkenness night after night, sometimes quarreling so viciously that they ended by physically beating one another.

Frightened and isolated from the rest of the family, the boy spoke to no one about his parents' behavior. To report to his brothers and sisters, he believed, would be a betrayal of his parents. And, then, turning to the others would only reinforce their view of him as the "baby" in the family, too young and not man enough to handle problems. Wayne's brief attempt at running away had been his first outward expression of his crushing unhappiness. But it had brought no changes in his family life, and had left him feeling guilty and ashamed. As the situation continued to deteriorate and Wayne felt more trapped annd helpless, he tried to end his life.

Both Mary and Wayne suffered from the hopelessness and despondency of the depressed. In both cases depressed feelings became masked by misleading behavior. Mary suffered physical symptoms that seemed, for a long time, far removed from emotional problems. And Wayne acted the role of a rebellious runaway, and then of a contrite and dutiful son, until he could bear no more and tried to kill himself.

The lines between masked depression and true clinical depression are not always clear-cut. A young person may alternate between angry and destructive behavior on the one hand and silent withdrawals on the other, or between boisterous showing off one day and tearful hours of loneliness the next. Generally, experts say, older teenagers—the eighteen- and nineteen-year-olds—more often show classic symptoms of depression typical of adults than do the younger teenagers between the ages of fourteen and eighteen. Younger boys and girls tend to camouflage their feelings more with impulsive and angry behavior. And they tend, too, toward suicide attempts that are more open appeals for help than true efforts to destroy themselves.

Too often parents, teachers, friends, and even physicians miss the urgent messages behind the frantic and sometimes infuriating actions of despairing teenagers. Ignored and untreated, these young people become more unhappy as they grow older. They may take up more destructive and antisocial activities that eventually lead them into trouble with the law. At the same time, their despondency may deepen and harden and their suicide attempts become aimed more surely at death.

Nobody who has studied depression has yet been able to point to one single cause and say: "This brings on clinical depression." Depression in different people may come from different causes. Many older people suffer clinical depression as a result of chemical changes within their bodies. Such people usually feel better quickly by taking tranquilizers and antidepressant drugs, and sometimes undergoing brief psychotherapy. Severe mental illness may cause depression in other people. Here, too, biochemical treatment often brings quick improvement. And then, for many people depression stems from emotional stresses that leave victims feeling deeply and desperately unhappy. In these cases intensive psychotherapy, often combined with antidepressant drugs, can help change a clinically depressed person's outlook on life.

At the root of many emotionally caused depressions lies a profound sense of loss, of someone or something that has been deeply loved. A depressed person may have lost something real, as in the loss of a parent or the loss of a job. Or the person may have experienced the loss of a special feeling or a state of being, such as the loss of power on a job or the loss of feeling needed and wanted. In either case the loss is so significant to the person that it leads to overwhelming sorrow along with feelings of weakness and unworthiness.

Young people may experience many kinds of painful losses. A child suffers terribly from the actual loss of a parent. Some studies have shown that if a child is not helped to handle the despair of losing a parent during the early years of life that child may suffer severe depression and suicidal thoughts in later years. A child whose parent dies experiences what Robert Jay Lifton calls "survivor guilt." Frightened and confused, the child wonders why he or she remained alive while the parent died. Sometimes the child becomes angry at the parent who has abandoned the family so abruptly, and then, terrified and guilty at having such feelings, directs the anger inward. During adolescence, when the young person goes through many other emotional and physical changes, the complex feelings of loss experienced in childhood may erupt again and lead to serious depression.

Perhaps even more crippling to a young person than the physical loss of a parent is the sense of love lost, of being unloved and uncared for. Children who grow up feeling unloved view themselves as unworthy of love. They feel useless and inept, and they turn against themselves and the world.

The way young people experience loss of love influences their reactions, according to Samuel C. Klagsbrun, a psychiatrist who has treated many children and young adults. Children who have received little love from their earliest days have, in a sense, lost love before they've even found it. These children grow up as deadened and morose adolescents and adults. They may retreat into a fantasy world, isolate themselves from others, and become "loners" incapable of giving or receiving love. In the most severe cases, they become seriously depressed and suicidal, allowing nobody to intrude on their lonely world. Children who have enjoyed some love in early life and then suffered the loss of that love—through death, divorce, or the breakup of a family—may show other forms of depression as they grow older. They may become enraged at the parents who loved them and left them, and then turn that rage inward against themselves. Such young people often get into violent arguments with their parents, become disruptive in school, and, in some cases, become serious juvenile delinquents. Tragically, their very anger and hurtful actions usually lead to greater rejection by parents and friends. And this rejection, in turn, pushes the person further into depression, and often into suicide.

Another kind of loss, a sad, unrelenting loss, also can lead to serious depression and suicidal thoughts among the young. This is the loss of physical health, and with it, the view of oneself as a complete and wholesome person.

The case of Brian G. illustrates the destructive effects of such a loss. A strong, athletic boy of thirteen, Brian began to sense a weakness and persistent pain in his right leg. Medical tests in a hospital led to the dread diagnosis of bone cancer. Doctors considered the cancer controllable, although not curable, and put Brian on a program of drug therapy. The boy handled the bad news well, and cooperated fully with the hospital staff that cared for him. After he returned home, however, Brian became irritable and listless, picking fights with his younger brother and provoking his parents, who went out of their way not to upset him. He refused to go to school, and spent hours alone in his room, with his record player and his books.

Puzzled and frightened, Brian's parents consulted a psychotherapist, who managed to meet with the boy and win his confidence. During their meetings, Brian revealed a deep-seated depression, which stemmed less from the actual illness than from the consequences of being ill. Once a leader in his group, Brian now saw himself as a weak and pathetic object of pity for his friends and family. He had lost his way of life and his proud image of himself. And, as in other losses leading to depression, he held himself somehow

47

responsible for his unhappy position. More than anything, Brian wanted to be as he had been before his illness. Yet he knew he never would be, and found himself incapable of handling that knowledge. Only after many weeks of therapy was Brian able to deal openly with his feeling of loss and emptiness. Then he began to resume a normal life that included living with the realities of his illness.

Of all the losses teenagers might suffer, the one that affects the greatest number is a sense of lost identity. In some ways the teen years themselves can be viewed as a time of just such a loss, a time that can lead to confused, depressive feelings.

During their adolescent years, girls and boys make their first real breaks with home and family. They begin to pull away from their parents, to venture out on their own and experience the world for themselves. As they move into their upper teens, they go off to college or leave home to get jobs and live by themselves. During these same teen years, young people lose their lifelong image of themselves. Their voices change, their bodies change and their interests change. Sexual feelings become aroused in ways they have never been aroused before and are not likely to be aroused again, and the young begin exploring their own sexuality and establishing their own sexual identities. Almost overnight, it seems, the child that once was turns into an almost-but-not-quite-adult person.

These changes in body and changes in lifestyles are exciting to young people and longed for by them. But they also bring great anxieties and moodswings. Torn between the bright, shining world of childhood and the challenging, unfamiliar world of adulthood, the young become frightened at times, dejected, and angry at themselves and the threatening outside. They also become preoccupied with thoughts of death and dying. They wonder about death as they wonder about many aspects of life they previously had taken for granted. They play with thoughts of death, and enjoy a sense of power in the knowledge that they can control the time and place of their own death. But many teenagers and young adults—well into their twenties —have an unrealistic view of death. In their mind's eye they see themselves as wrapped in a cloak of immortality. Even those who attempt suicide usually lack a true concept of the finality of death.

Their fascination with death along with the tensions of adolescence make young people especially vulnerable to depression and to dark, self-destructive thoughts. Most of the young, of course, pass through adolescence and go on to live productive adult lives. But for those who receive little understanding, who feel alone and isolated with no base of love and support upon which to build, the confusions and conflicts of adolescence can be overwhelming. These young people find themselves becoming "square inside . . . and brown," crushed by sadness and the lonely nightmare of clinical depression.

4 The Mentally Ill

|||||⊏]||||||||||||⊏]||||||||||⊏]||||||||||⊏]||||||||||⊏]||||||||||⊏]||||||||||⊏]||||||||||⊏]||||||||||⊏]||||||||||⊏]|||||||||⊏]|||||

When Psychosis Leads to Suicide

NEW HAVEN BOY, 16, KILLS PARENTS WITH AX THEN LEAPS TO DEATH OFF BUILDING ROOF

The newspaper headlines on a cold Monday morning in March blared out the grisly story of Peter W. The teenager and his parents had spent a quiet weekend in their large old frame house in the heart of New Haven, Connecticut. On Sunday evening they ate dinner together at a local restaurant, whose owner had seen them many times. Back home, Peter went to his room to prepare his homework while his parents sat in the living room watching television. About 10 o'clock Peter entered the living room and attacked his father from behind with a two-foot ax, murdering him after several blows. He grabbed his mother as she ran from the room, and turned his ax on her too.

A few minutes after the double murder the boy walked several blocks to a high-rise building where a friend lived. The doorman recognized him and joked with him as he entered the building. Peter took the elevator to the top floor, then climbed a flight of steps to the roof. From there he jumped to his death.

In a refrain of astonishment that often follows such horror stories, friends, neighbors, and teachers expressed disbelief that sweet, charming Peter could commit such crimes. "There were no red flags," said the headmaster of the private high school Peter attended. "Peter had no problems."

Just how wrong the headmaster and the neighbors were became evident from investigations by police and the medical examiner's office. The boy who "had no problems," they discovered, led a secret life of brutality and sadistic fantasy that centered around a secret closet behind a panel in his bedroom wall. Shelves lined the sides of the closet, and on each shelf lay stacks of magazine and newspaper clippings along with photographs, leaflets and hand-written manuscripts. The motifs throughout were the same: brutal murders, sadistic sexual practices, Nazi atrocities, and vicious anti-black and anti-Jewish hate messages. Nazi armbands and a heavily marked copy of Adolf Hitler's *Mein Kampf* held a place of honor on the center shelf.

None of Peter's friends knew of his secret cache of papers and pictures. And neither they nor experts who studied the case could say with certainty what part the closet filled with hate had played in Peter's life. Perhaps he imagined himself a superman in the image the Nazis tried to build for themselves, brutalizing weaker people and lording over all who, in real life, frightened and dominated him. Or perhaps in his fantasies he vacillated between the roles of oppressor and victim, with each offering satisfaction in different ways. What did become clear in the investigation into Peter's world was that his escape into unreality somehow eased the pressures and anxieties he carried around with him constantly, like a weight about his neck.

Careful questioning of friends and teachers revealed that Peter felt driven to achieve well in school. His parents had pulled themselves up from poverty to a respected upper-middle-class standing in their commu-

51

nity. They had high expectations, of which Peter was always aware. Although the pressures Peter's parents placed on him may not have been stronger than those in other families, Peter himself felt an enormous need to succeed in order to please them. He worried all the time about grades, and went into a tailspin of depression at even the slightest hint of criticism by a teacher.

One of Peter's few close friends recalled that a few days before the tragedy, a math teacher had reprimanded Peter for sloppy homework. The boy had spoken again and again of the incident during those days. "I hope he doesn't tell my parents," he repeated daily, although the teacher had never suggested he would. "If he tells my parents I'll have to kill myself," Peter told his friend. Knowing Peter's overanxious attitude toward school, the friend paid little attention to the worries or the threat.

Peter's uncle remembered too that on occasion he had seen Peter have uncontrollable temper tantrums, in which the boy raged and cursed at his parents, threw things about, and banged his fists against the wall. The strange thing, said the uncle, was that when a tantrum ended, Peter would go to his room for awhile and then return calm and smiling with no apparent recollection of the incident.

What happened to Peter on that fatal Sunday night? Nobody can be sure. Experts who investigated the case agreed, however, that Peter was hounded by worries and tensions that, because of his own personality and temperament, he could not handle. While on the surface he maintained a normal life, within himself he inhabited a tormented world filled with anger and hatred. When internal pressures reached a bursting point, he lost hold of the real world altogether. For reasons that had more to do with his fantasies than with actual causes, he destroyed his parents and himself, every aspect of the life he could no longer bear.

Peter was plagued by severe mental illness, technically called psychosis. People who suffer such illnesses are known as psychotics. You may get the impression from reading newspaper stories of sensational or bizarre suicides that anyone who commits suicide is psychotic or "mad." Actually, most people who become suicidal do not suffer from psychotic illnesses. Most suicides and attempted suicides result from deep depression and sometimes from neurotic disturbances that are less severe than psychotic ones. But some suicides do come about as a direct result of psychotic illnesses. Although these illnesses are serious and dangerous, many can be controlled if treated early, and suicides can be prevented.

The underlying feature of all psychotic illnesses is a break with reality. Psychotic people lose the ability to distinguish between what is happening and what they imagine is happening. They act out their fantasies, unaware that their actions seem strange and disorganized to others. Most psychotics have lucid periods, however, when the clouds of confusion lift for awhile. And many can live relatively normal lives until some event leads to an open break with reality. Peter, for example, functioned so well in his everyday life that nobody suspected he had created a twisted and tortured inner world for himself.

Some psychotic illnesses result from organic causes, such as brain damage in early childhood. Some come about because of biochemical imbalances in the body that may be inherited or may develop over the course of years. And many have psychological or emotional causes that stem from disturbed family relationships. Doctors usually treat psychotic illnesses with drugs, often combined with psychotherapy, and sometimes using family therapy that involves parents and other relatives.

Among the greatest dangers in psychotic illnesses is

that others either do not recognize when a person has become mentally sick, or do not allow themselves to acknowledge the sickness. Often those close to a disturbed person become caught up in that person's distortions of reality, mostly because they cannot bring themselves to believe the person can be mentally ill.

In one situation, a high school boy kept telling his girlfriend that all his teachers had joined in a plot against him. Although he knew every answer on his exams, he said, he continually received failing grades. The teachers, he confided, failed him because they feared the power he would hold over them if he received the high grades he deserved. The story sounded strange to the girl. But then again, she reasoned, he spoke so convincingly that what he said *could* be true. When the boy accused her of being part of the plot, she finally faced the fact that he had become mentally sick.

If you suspect that someone you know is mentally disturbed, act on your suspicions, tell parents, teachers, or other friends about your feelings, and try to get help for that person. The longer a psychotic illness continues, the more difficult it may be to treat.

Young people may suffer from a number of different kinds of psychotic illnesses that have strong suicidal components. One that often strikes during the early or middle teen years is schizophrenia. In its early stages the symptoms of this disease may be hardly noticeable. A schizophrenic girl or boy may act somewhat withdrawn and moody, but otherwise not appear much different from other teenagers. As the disease progresses, however, schizophrenics withdraw further within themselves, sometimes becoming so withdrawn that they become oblivious to anything about them. Many have hallucinations or hear voices that command them to act. Sometimes they speak out loud to their voices, and laugh or cry because of things the voices tell them. Schizophrenics may react with great anger or violence to the slightest degree of frustration or the tiniest sign of disapproval by others. Many have delusions in which they become so fixed on some illogical thought or false idea that no amount of reasoning can sway their thinking.

For some young schizophrenics the illness itself, with its escape to an inner world, serves as a protection against suicide. For others the break with reality, often mixed with overpowering depression, can lead to an elaborate system of beliefs and fantasies that bring about self-destruction. In a few relatively rare cases, such as that of Peter W., their twisted reasoning leads schizophrenics to suddenly attack or murder others and then turn around and kill themselves.

More typical of schizophrenia among the young than Peter's case is the history of Melanie J. By the age of sixteen, Melanie knew with certainty that she hated her mother and loved her father. She had good reasons to support her feelings. A driving, demanding, unloving woman, Melanie's mother pressed her daughter into becoming the embodiment of all her hopes in life. The slightest shortcoming in Melanie brought forth furious criticisms or mocking insults from her mother.

Melanie's father learned early in his marriage not to interfere with his wife. A gentle, scholarly man, he loved his daughter in an absent-minded way, teasing her and indulging her but rarely taking her seriously. She, however, idolized him. In her fantasies he became her savior, her friend and lover, her husband and brother as well as her father.

Filled with hatred for her mother, yet torn with guilt over those feelings and over her equally passionate love for her father, Melanie tried to live the life of perfection her mother had planned for her. She excelled in her studies, became proficient in music, and was praised by teachers and friends. Inwardly she built an elaborate world of anger, fear, and guilt. She kept a "book of deeds" in which she listed every grievance she had against her mother. As the list grew she began to harbor within her a chorus of secret voices. Sometimes the voices told her to kill her mother. And sometimes they berated her in her mother's familiar mocking tones.

With the help of her voices Melanie gradually developed a complex solution to her life's problems. Using the number eight as a base, she decided that at age sixteen she already had lived out two-thirds of her life. She would allow herself to live another eight years, until she turned twenty-four. If the quality of her life did not improve by then, she would kill herself on her twenty-fourth birthday.

As Melanie's inner world became more intricate her outer world began to fall apart. Time and again the model student fell asleep at exams. Time and again the talented pianist took sick moments before a recital, or left her music at home, or simply forgot her pieces. Furious at her daughter's increasing failures, Melanie's mother insisted that the girl see a psychiatrist to cure her "forgetfulness." Although she raged inwardly, Melanie conformed to her mother's wishes.

Melanie liked her psychiatrist because he reminded her of her father. He prescribed medication to relieve some of her anxieties, and he met with her regularly to talk about her problems and feelings. As she began to gain new insights into her relationships with her parents, she was able to give up her inner voices and cope openly with many of her conflicts.

But Melanie held tightly to her mathematical formulation of life and her plan to kill herself at age twenty-four. To prove her seriousness, she carried a razor with her always. Sometimes, just seconds before entering her psychiatrist's office, she made thin cuts along her wrists so that her hands dripped blood as her session began. Her suicide gesture served as a warning: "No matter how much you influence me, I still have control over my own life and death."

A few times Melanie made halfhearted suicide attempts that led to brief hospitalizations. After each attempt she seemed almost renewed, free of tensions and ready to pursue her shaky road to health. Melanie made her last suicide attempt when she was twenty. This time she swallowed a massive dose of aspirin, and was rushed to a hospital in coma. After she recovered, Melanie spoke of her disappointment in herself and of the wasted years of her life. But she never spoke again of killing herself. Having come close to dying she no longer saw death as a solution to life's problems. She continued her therapy, working seriously to become well. On her twenty-fourth birthday she sent her therapist a happy birthday card.

Melanie had suffered much emotional damage in her early life, and she spent many years in therapy undoing that damage. In spite of the seriousness of her illness, she was able to recover and live a full and productive life. Many schizophrenics are not that lucky. Undiagnosed and untreated, or treated inadequately, their distorted habits and ideas become too fixed to be changed. Some spend years of their lives in and out of mental institutions. Others destroy themselves while still in their teens.

In Sean C.'s case therapy came too late and too superficially to stay the drive toward self-destruction. Sean suffered from a different kind of mental illness than Melanie, a type of schizophrenia known as paranoid schizophrenia. People with this illness become exceptionally suspicious of everyone and everything around them. As their illness intensifies they may believe that all the people they know have become involved in a diabolic plot to destroy them.

57

At the height of his illness, Sean felt convinced that even the planes flying overhead had been sent by a secret agency to check on him. He refused to speak to his parents or friends for fear they would reveal to "high officials" the innermost workings of his mind. He withdrew instead into himself, communicating silently with the voices he heard and the images he saw before him.

A brilliant student, Sean had his first psychotic breakdown during his senior year in high school. Screaming with fear then, he had tried to kill himself to escape the hounding voices he heard within him, accusing him of evil and impurity. He was hospitalized and recovered sufficiently to graduate from high school and begin college. He saw several therapists, one after another, after he left the hospital, but could not relate to any of them and soon stopped all treatment.

During his first year at college the tensions within him began to mount once more. And again he became immersed in a world of suspicions and fears and accusing voices. He had several breakdowns and made a series of suicide attempts. During his final breakdown Sean escaped from the hospital to which he had been sent, ran home to his twelfth-floor apartment, and dove out the window to his death.

At the root of Sean's private hell lay a frightening attachment to his mother. Combined with this was a strong dislike of his father mixed with a childlike yearning to be loved and accepted by the older man. Sean adored his beautiful and accomplished mother, and she returned his affection full-heartedly. The two were almost inseparable, sharing mutual interests in art, music, and literature. Their closeness left no room for Sean's hard-headed businessman father, who, in turn, held himself aloof from his son.

As he approached his mid-teens Sean became painfully aware of his great dependence on his mother, and terrified by sexual fantasies he had about her. At the same time he became deeply disturbed by a growing sense of homosexual longing within himself. He abhorred homosexuality. In his mind he could see his mother's look of disgust as they passed hand-holding homosexual couples on the city streets. Yet every day homosexual dreams tugged at his mind.

Pulled in many directions, Sean could not explain his fears and confusions to his mother or reach out to his father, the one man who might help him. He retreated into himself, trusting nobody. Over time his arena of suspicion and distrust spread ever outward, until it encompassed even his beloved mother. In the end Sean died isolated and cut off from the real world, accompanied only by his tormenting inner voices and images.

Another kind of psychotic illness that, untreated, may lead to suicidal thoughts and actions is manic-depressive psychosis. People with this disease swing in mood between great heights of emotion and profound depths of despair. The sickness may begin during the teen years or early twenties and continue throughout life. Physicians suspect that it originates from biochemical causes within the body. They usually treat it with a drug called lithium, which keeps the disease in check and helps patients live a normal life.

During the manic phase of the illness, the person feels constantly high and happy, euphoric about all aspects of life. A manic person may use the simplest event—a rainstorm, a train ride—as a takeoff for ecstatic expressions of joy and wonder. Mixed with their wild happiness, manic people often become edgy or suspicious of others. They burst easily into anger, and find themselves involved in violent arguments over small, sometimes imagined insults.

During the depressive part of the illness, anger and violence fade along with good cheer. The person moves

59

into dark despondency, haunted by pounding thoughts of suicide. As the depression becomes more pronounced, suicidal dangers loom larger. Now family and friends need to be cautiously alert to suicidal talks and hints of death wishes.

At various stages in different psychotic illnesses, symptoms may overlap, and even professionals have difficulty diagnosing the exact nature of the illness. A lay person shouldn't try to make distinctions. The best you can do is be aware if a friend or relative begins to act in ways that seem disoriented or irrational to you. Try to get help for that person by involving close family members in the problem and seeking professional advice.

5 Uncounted Suicides

How People Kill Themselves Without "Committing Suicide"

"I had been taking drugs since I was fifteen. During this time I made two suicide attempts by slitting my wrists. The first time I was high on downs and feeling sorry for myself. I just wanted attention. I didn't really want to die. The second time I was very depressed. I was hooking for drug money on and off for almost two years and it just got to me. In looking back at this attempt I think I really wanted to die. My life was nothing but drugs and unhappiness and more drugs. Right after this I sought help and enrolled in the methadone program. I haven't taken heroin since then, and I have no desire to kill myself . . .

"I had a friend who used to deal in heroin. Then a dope drought came to the city and he had to stop dealing, so he lost a lot of income. He used to spend his money on drugs, drinking, and girls. Another girl and I were the last of his friends to see him alive. It was a hot summer night in August. The three of us were hanging around across the street from the apartment house in which he lived. He said he felt tired and left. We knew he had been drinking wine and smoking, and that he took some downs, but we didn't know that he also had taken methadone. His mother found him in bed the next morning. She called for help but it was too late. He had died some time during the night. Such a damn waste of life. By the way, he was only eighteen."

These descriptions of her own suicide attempts and the death of her friend were written by a college student in response to this author's questionnaire about suicide sent to high school and college students. She wrote with integrity about a life that revolved around drugs, a life in which death and suicide become everyday occurrences. Like her, thousands of other teenagers who have plunged deep into the drug scene live on the outskirts of death. A few, like her, give up drugs after awhile. Many others spend their lives in and out of jail, in and out of treatment centers, in a revolving-door routine that leads nowhere. And many die; some suddenly, as this girl's friend did, of an overdose or fatal combination of drugs; others experience the slow death of mental and physical deterioration.

Thousands of other young people drink themselves into stupors with liquor or wine or some combination of drugs and liquor. Some attempt or commit suicide because of their drinking, and some become deathly ill with kidney or liver diseases. And then too, thousands of people die or become disfigured as a result of accidents as they speed along highways or carelessly go about the business of their lives.

Behind them all—the drug freaks, the alcoholics, the careless drivers—hovers the specter of death. In dozens of ways they play with death, they challenge death, and often they seek death. When they do die from their drugs or drinking or driving, their deaths are not counted into official lists of suicide statistics. But you would not be wrong to say that many of these people destroyed themselves, as surely as did those who openly committed suicide.

Everybody acts in self-destructive or self-defeating ways at times. You receive an invitation to a party that you know you don't want to attend. But you say "yes" because you can't bring yourself to say "no," and then you spend the entire evening at the party feeling angry and resentful. Or you work late into the night preparing an important research assignment. Then you forget to bring your report to class the next day, and receive a failing grade on the assignment.

Sigmund Freud, who first described how the unconscious mind works, said that all people have unconscious wishes to hurt themselves, punish themselves, or even destroy themselves in various ways. Many of the poor decisions people make or the inappropriate things they say and do that appear to happen by chance really reflect these hidden, self-destructive wishes. In some people, said Freud, unconscious needs for self-punishment go far beyond the norm, leading to dangerous self-destructive acts. Freud told the story of a Mr. K., who had been the lover of Freud's patient Dora. After their affair broke up Dora turned violently against Mr. K., accusing him of having hurt her deeply. One day the two accidentally met in a busy section of town. Stunned to see Dora, Mr. K. stepped into the busy street and, according to Freud, "allowed himself to be knocked down by a car." Poor Mr. K., torn with guilt and pain over Dora's accusations, unconsciously tried to kill himself by getting in the way of the car.

The many unconscious ways people destroy themselves became the subject of a fascinating book by Karl Menninger, one of Freud's most ardent followers. In the book *Man Against Himself* Menninger pointed out that people who do dangerously self-destructive things may unconsciously want to die without having to take responsibility for killing themselves. He described drug addicts and alcoholics as "chronic suicides" who destroy themselves slowly, always on the pretext of making life more bearable. Other kinds of self-destructive people whom Menninger studied included the accident-prone who seem to bring accidents on themselves and hypochondriacs who constantly undergo painful medical treatment or surgery when they really suffer no serious illnesses.

We see dozens of examples in everyday life of the kind of uncounted suicides Menninger described. Teenage girls, and occasionally boys, go on fad diets to lose weight and sometimes become so obsessed with the idea of being skinny that they come close to starving themselves. People with long-term illnesses, such as diabetes, consistently "forget" to take their medication, and become dangerously sick as a result. Other people refuse to see a doctor or get a medical checkup even when—or especially when—they suspect they may have a serious problem. More commonly, people smoke three or four packs of cigarettes a day although study after study has linked cigarette smoking with lung cancer.

In most of these situations nobody thinks to connect the destructive behavior directly to suicide. Everybody cheers on the compulsive young dieter and praises her willpower long after somebody should have noticed her emaciated looks and symptoms of malnutrition. Young high school students look up to classmates who have become expert smokers, and can hardly wait to achieve their supposed sophistication and maturity. Teenagers speak admiringly of friends who drive quickly and recklessly. And even in wildly life-threatening situations, many hidden suicides get adulation and praise. Thousands paid top prices to watch Evel Knievel hurtle himself on his motorcycle across huge canyons and chasms. Some even tried to imitate him, dying in the attempt.

When somebody attempts suicide, the underlying threat of death is obvious. But many people who constantly do things to hurt themselves do not consciously realize the dangers of their actions, or do not want to face them. These people often need the care and concern of others as much as do those who openly try to kill themselves. At the very least they need to have someone whom they respect point out to them just how they are destroying themselves, and how they can get help for their problems.

Most widespread of the destructive activities young people take part in are drug abuse, alcoholism, and reckless driving. Each has much in common with suicidal behavior, and can be related to it.

Drug abuse and suicide are closely linked. Like suicidal acts, drug abuse is a symptom of deep psychological pain. From studies of young drug abusers we know that these people suffer almost unbearable despondency. They hate themselves and feel useless and worthless, much the way suicide attempters do. Rather than choosing outright suicide, many drug abusers chip away at their lives, dying slowly, little by little. Others alternate between deadening themselves with drugs and seeking actual death through suicide.

Different kinds of drugs seem to appeal to people with different kinds of emotional problems. Psychiatrist Herbert Hendin studied men and women students abusing many kinds of drugs as part of a larger psychoanalytic study of Columbia University students he conducted for his book *The Age of Sensation*. Although many drug abusers in the study mixed the drugs they used, many others tended to favor one or another group of drugs according to their own emotional needs. For example, students who got stoned on marijuana every day shared basic problems that related to feelings of aggressiveness and competitiveness. For the most part, these students came from families that stressed competition and high achievements. The students themselves had overpowering competitive feelings, but they resented those feelings, which they knew their parents had instilled in them. They used marijuana to cut down their aggressive and competitive drives and at the same time to revolt against pressures from their parents to succeed.

Unlike the marijuana abusers the LSD and psychedelic users did not want simply to temper their emotions, but rather to escape beyond all emotions and feelings. Most of these students had grown up feeling rejected and lonely, never allowing themselves to become close to others because of the pain that might result. They used LSD to "blow their minds" and open up new worlds of experience. But their new worlds and their mind-blowing experiences served all the while to push away their emotions, to shelter them from the rage and despair they might feel if they permitted themselves to feel anything.

Amphetamine abusers escaped their feelings in a different way. Women made up the vast majority of amphetamine users seen in this study. Almost all felt an urgent need to please their parents and fulfill goals their parents had set for them. Brought up to ignore their needs and please others, they kept themselves high on amphetamines, "speeding" through their days with no time left to think about how they felt or what they wanted. Having destroyed their true selves, these young women programmed themselves to be efficient machines. But at times when the programming failed and the machinery broke down, they became openly suicidal.

Of all the drug abusers in the study, heroin users came across as the most despairing and self-destructive.

These students had been deeply hurt early in their lives. Now to prevent further hurt, they plied themselves with drugs, dulling all feelings and keeping the world, their parents, their friends, and even themselves at a distance.

In addition to the slowly self-destructive aspects of drugs themselves, drug abuse often leads more directly to suicide and death. Young people have killed themselves during bad LSD trips, impulsively, with little awareness of what they were doing. Others have become psychotic and out of touch with reality, killing themselves because of their delusions of great power and omnipotence. And others, especially heroin and narcotics users, gamble with death again and again, knowing full well that each shot can lead to fatal infection, each fix be adulterated and lethal. They gamble because life holds little meaning to them. Yet, paradoxicallly, their disregard for life gives them a feeling of invulnerability, as though just because they don't care, nothing can happen to them. Often, however, when even drugged numbness does not block out the emotional pain that torments them, they use their drug to kill themselves.

A well-known addict who gambled with heroin, and lost, was the rock singer Janis Joplin. She died at age twenty-seven on October 4, 1970.

All her life Janis seemed to struggle and suffer. She grew up in the small town of Port Arthur, Texas, where quiet conformity served as the keynote to success. But Janis could never conform. As a teenager she became fat and unattractive, with a severe case of acne and a deriding manner that put others off. By the time she reached the University of Texas, she looked so unattractive to her classmates that they nominated her for the title "Ugliest Man on Campus."

Janis ran away from the hurt and humiliation she suffered into the heart of the drug and hippie scene in San Francisco. She became part of that scene, getting high on "speed" and shooting heroin to ease the lows. She also began dealing in dope to support her habit. During the next few years she traveled back and forth between the West Coast and the East, on and off drugs, on and off alcohol, living a partially homosexual life, but trying desperately to be "straight."

Even while she grappled with her problems, Janis blossomed professionally. By the late 1960s she had become acclaimed as a first-rate rock blues singer. When she performed she worked her audience into a frenzy of feeling, sharing with them a wild, frenetic musical "trip." Yet she was constantly gnawed by the fear that her thousands of adulating fans would one day decide she was a phony. "I go to bed worrying and I wake up worrying every morning that they'll have found out I really can't sing," she told Myra Friedman, who later described her life in the biography *Buried Alive*.

Throughout the few short years of her fame, she drank heavily, went on heroin, and then prided herself for going off the drug. As time went on her drinking became heavier and the underlying despair and loneliness that always plagued her began to surface more and more. During the months before she died she spoke several times of suicide and of her fantasies of ending her life. A few weeks before her death she began shooting heroin again.

Janis died of an overdose of heroin, officially listed as an accident by the coroner. Nobody will ever know just how large a part accident played and how much a wish to die influenced that last, fatal shot. It almost makes no difference; Janis had headed toward self-destruction for years.

Long before she became entangled in the heroin trap, Janis Joplin had been drinking heavily. Typical of many heavy drinkers, she was torn by self-doubts and insecurities in spite of her enormous talents. And like so many other alcoholics she wanted more than anything to be loved.

People who become problem drinkers are often people who feel deprived of love. They suffer throughout their lives for a love they believe they had been cheated of in childhood. They try to anesthetize themselves with alcohol, to dull the hurt and longing they feel. In the process they become caught up in a form of self-destruction that may cause more pain than the sorrow it supposedly relieves.

Alcohol has misleading effects. People who drink feel better for awhile. They forget their problems and become carefree and high. But alcohol cannot truly relieve depression, because it is a depressant itself. After the first happy flush wears off, the drinker feels lower than before, saddled now with the additional burdens of guilt and remorse for having drunk so much. The renewed depression may start the cycle going again. In some people this pattern of depression, drinking, and more depression may continue for years. If these people do not get help for their problem they may alienate family and friends and find themselves more isolated and depressed than ever. Overwhelmed by their depression, they often turn to suicide.

The suicide rate among alcoholics is an astonishing fifty-eight times higher than it is among the normal population. And about one of every three suicides in the population as a whole is related to alcohol in some way. Either the suicidal person was an alcoholic; or the person mixed alcohol with barbiturates as the method of suicide; or the person drank a large quantity of alcohol before committing suicide, perhaps to temper the fear of death; or the person committed suicide impulsively or accidentally in a foggy state of mind as a result of drinking too much.

Less directly, chronic alcoholism, like chronic drug abuse, is a slow form of suicide. People often think of chronic alcoholics as men and women in their thirties and forties who drink because of the emptiness and failures of their lives. But the astounding increase in drinking among teenagers and pre-teens in the 1970s has brought about a group of teenage alcoholics who are slowly destroying themselves.

It is shocking to learn that almost one of every five teenagers in the United States can be classified as a problem drinker, drinking regularly and becoming drunk at least six times a year. Among thirteen-year-olds, one of every four drinks moderately, and that is in spite of the fact that the legal drinking age in every state is at least eighteen! These figures were compiled by a survey made for the National Institute of Alcohol Abuse and Alcoholism, and published in 1978.

A child who begins drinking at age twelve or less may be headed for a course of self-destruction from which there is no turning back. Such a child was Juan A. When nineteen-year-old Juan appeared at the emergency room of a large city hospital, nobody knew of his alcoholism. The young man had been rushed to the hospital after nearly chopping off his arm in a vicious accident at the machine shop in which he worked.

Surgeons operated on Juan's arm and placed him in the surgery ward to recuperate. His arm began to heal nicely, but the patient showed other symptoms of severe illness that puzzled the staff. He twisted and turned in violent, uncontrollable convulsions. He ran a fever, screamed out in horror periodically, and jumped with terror whenever someone approached his bed or made the slightest noise. He also reported seeing wild and frightening images to whom he spoke incoherently.

Juan suffered from delirium tremens, the racking convulsions and hallucinations that torture alcoholics when their alcohol is suddenly withdrawn. The surgery staff quickly sent him to the detoxification unit of the hospital to be treated for his alcoholism. Doctors and nurses there found him to be emaciated and jaundiced, suffering from cirrhosis of the liver and severe malnutrition. Along with his medical treatment, they gave him psychiatric care.

Juan told a tragic story. His mother had died shortly after his birth. His parents had never married, and he did not know his father. With great resentment, his mother's sister allowed the infant to live with her. Over the years she had seven children of her own, but she never treated Juan as one of her family. Instead, she made a servant of him, ordering him to care for the other children and help in the household.

When he was about twelve years old Juan started drinking beer and cheap liquor with some of his friends. He quickly became the heaviest drinker in the group, continuing in the evenings long after the others returned home. Most nights he could barely drag his body to his room, and when he did, he drank himself into a stupor. Juan's aunt threw him out of her home when he was sixteen. He moved in with a friend, and supported himself with odd jobs. Often he panhandled, and sometimes he mugged neighborhood children to get money for liquor. Just a month before his accident, he took a job at the machine shop.

After several weeks on the detoxification unit Juan felt well enough to be released from the hospital. He had gained weight, and talked of staying off "booze" for good. But as he walked away to resume his rootless life, the hospital staff knew his prognosis for success was bleak. He would be back on liquor quickly, they suspected, and would probably drink himself to death before he reached thirty.

Of all the self-destructive activities young people take part in, reckless driving carries the most immediate dangers to life. Traffic accidents kill more young people between the ages of fifteen and twenty-four than any other cause of death. Every year more than 18,000 teenagers and young adults die in such accidents, about twice as many as die from all other accidents combined. In fact teenagers get into far more traffic accidents than do adults, and are more often killed or seriously injured in accidents.

We know that many deaths recorded as accidents are actually disguised suicides. If the cause of death is not clear, coroners usually list the death as an accident, giving the family the benefit of the doubt. When a death comes about as a result of a traffic accident, officials rarely rule it suicide even when evidence points in that direction. In one case a sixteen-year-old unmarried pregnant girl was hit by a car and instantly killed. The medical examiner ruled the death an accident even though a witness swore he had seen the girl hide behind a tree and jump in front of the car as it sped toward her.

Most fatal car accidents are not intentional suicides, but often the people involved have unconscious needs to hurt themselves, or they become careless with their lives because of pressing emotional problems. Driver education courses rarely mention the importance of emotions in driving. Yet recognizing how personality traits can influence driving habits and how a driver's worries and anxieties can contribute to road accidents is as important as recognizing road signs and signal lights.

To find out how people who have been in serious auto accidents compare in personality and thinking with suicidal people, psychiatrist Norman Tabachnick and some colleagues at the Los Angeles Suicide Prevention Center set up research projects into the psychology of fatal accidents.

The researchers found that about 25 percent of the accident victims they studied were depressed people with feelings of helplessness and a sense of loss typical of suicidal men and women. These people had had fantasies and dreams of death and self-destruction shortly before their accidents. The serious accidents they suffered may well have resulted from underlying wishes to destroy themselves.

Just the opposite traits, however, characterized the other 75 percent of accident cases studied. These people, most of them men, were tough and self-reliant with an image of themselves as strong and masculine. When under pressure or faced with a difficult problem, they acted quickly and impulsively, giving little thought to the consequences of their actions.

Many of the drivers in the sample were young men about to take on new responsibilities—enter college, begin a job, get married. They had felt anxious and uncertain about those responsibilities. They had responded to the challenges facing them by taking more risks, showing off more than usual, and being less cautious and attentive to detail. Their accidents had resulted from the emotional stress they felt and their responses to it.

Investigations into teenage driving habits have also pointed up the combined roles of personality traits and emotions in bringing about serious accidents. In one study two Dartmouth Medical School psychiatrists examined the driving records and family lives of 496 teenagers, aged sixteen to nineteen, in two rural counties of New Hampshire. They found that teenage boys likely to have accidents are usually outgoing, boisterous, rebellious people, careful to maintain a strong "macho" image of themselves. Under family pressure or the daily stresses of teen life, they become impulsive and careless drivers, often drinking before driving, and more interested in power and speed than in safety.

Accidents among girls, which occur far less frequently, come about more often from fatigue after many miles of driving than because of personality factors, the researchers found. We might guess that girls in our society feel freer to express their worries and unhappiness than boys, who often cover their emotions with bravado and "masculine" behavior that may lead to accidents.

Karl Menninger interpreted most accidents as the result of unconscious self-destructive drives. From the various studies that have been made more recently, it would appear that suicidal fantasies and wishes lie at the root of some traffic accidents, and that many others are connected with brash, impulsive behavior— a defiance of fate that Menninger might still classify as self-destructive.

The different ways accidents relate to suicide can be seen in the cases of two well-known accident victims, one who died in an auto crash and the other on a flying mission.

James Dean, the actor, was killed on September 30, 1955, en route to enter a road race in Salinas, California. Twenty-four-year-old Dean was speeding along in his new silver Porsche Spyder sports car, which he had bought especially for the race, when he failed to see another car turn out of a narrow intersection. He died instantly as the car hurled into him.

Thousands of teenage fans mourned Dean for years after his death. They identified with his rebelliousness and his defiance of the adult Establishment. Dean seemed in real life to be the epitome of the characters he played on the screen: the angry hero of *Rebel*

Without a Cause who chicken-races another boy in a car along the edge of a cliff; the arrogant, striving, and pathetic Jett Rink of *Giant* who comes from humble beginnings, grows wealthy and powerful, and in the end kills himself.

Dean, too, began humbly, in the small town of Fairmont, Indiana. His mother died when he was nine years old, and the boy grew up lonely, moody, and defiant. In Hollywood he became known for his sullen unfriendliness to people in power, his loyalty and warmth to a few close friends, and his willingness to stand his ground no matter what the consequences. If he disagreed with a director, he stormed off the set. If he quarreled with a producer, he quit a film. "If a choice is in order," he said in one of his last interviews, "I'd rather have people hiss than yawn."

Dean loved auto racing and fast driving. He liked the feeling of speed and strength that came to him as he zoomed along the track. And he liked to tempt death and to laugh at death. His favorite trick was to tie a hangman's noose tightly around his neck and then free himself, while frightened friends watched and cheered. He enjoyed the trick so much that he had a noose hung permanently in his living room.

When Dean died he had just completed work on the film *Giant*. "Dean died at just the right time," said actor Humphrey Bogart. "He left behind a legend. If he had lived, he'd never have been able to live up to his publicity."

French aviator and author Antoine de Saint-Exupéry did not have a following of hero-worshiping fans the way Dean did. But for those who knew his works, his death came as a great loss. And it remained a mysterious puzzle in which self-destructive thoughts and suicidal dreams may be the key pieces.

Saint-Exupéry was forty-four years old when he disappeared in his plane on July 31, 1944, in the midst

75

of World War II. He had taken off from an Allied airfield at Bastia in Corsica for a reconnaissance mission over France. He never returned and no trace of him was found.

An expert pilot, Saint-Exupéry was known as an aviation pioneer who opened new routes over Africa, the South Atlantic and the Andes Mountains. During World War II he successfully led a French squadron in an air fight with superior German forces. Yet, for all his skill, he became involved in a series of flying accidents that stemmed from his own carelessness. In one flight from Paris to Saigon in 1935 he took off unrested after a sleepless night and crashed into a sand dune on the Libyan desert. Just by chance a Bedouin found him and rescued him. Two years later, planning to fly from New York to Tierra del Fuego, he crashed on takeoff after unthinkingly overloading his plane with fuel. Several other minor accidents occurred before his final disappearance.

Saint-Exupéry's father died when the boy was four years old, and a beloved brother when he was seventeen. Throughout his life, and in the popular books that he wrote about flying, he seemed preoccupied with thoughts of death and with fantasies about himself as a savior and a hero.

In 1943, a year before his disappearance, he wrote *The Little Prince,* a book for children that has become a classic for adults too. Told in the first person, it recounts the adventures of a pilot whose plane has crashed in a desert. Alone with his damaged plane, the pilot is startled to meet a beautiful little boy who explains that he is the ruler and sole inhabitant of the planet Asteroid B-612. The two become good friends.

One day the pilot overhears the boy making an appointment with a yellow desert snake he has met. "You have good poison?" the boy asks the snake.

"You are sure that it will not make me suffer too long?"

Terrified, the pilot tries to keep the little prince from his appointment. But the child explains that the time has come for him to return to his own planet. He assures his friend that after the snake bites him he will only look dead, but he will not be dead. He will simply leave his body behind because it is too heavy to take with him. "But it will be like an old abandoned shell," he explains. "There is nothing sad about old shells."

With tears in his eyes the child tells the pilot that whenever the older man looks up to the sky he will find the stars laughing with the little prince's own laughter. And they will sound like "five hundred million little bells." Then the little prince goes off to meet the snake.

In the fantasy of *The Little Prince* Saint-Exupéry romanticized suicide as a form of "going home," and death as a painless process of shedding the body like "an old abandoned shell" while freeing the soul to soar to the skies. Did Saint-Exupéry set his own appointment with fate as he took off on his final mission? People who saw him before he left said he had complained of a sleepless night and seemed ressless and depressed. The evening before the flight he had prepared a letter in the form of a last will.

Was Saint Exupéry's death suicide or accident? Probably a combination of both.

Part Two:
What Can You Do?

6 The Suicidal Crisis

What Can You Do?

Two teenage girls taped the following discussion of their reactions to the suicide attempts of their friend Laurie K. Laurie's own description of one of her attempts appears at the beginning of Chapter 1. The girls spoke openly and frankly. Although Laurie listened in on the discussion, she said nothing.

Beth: "When Laurie first started slashing her wrists and things, most of us felt she was just trying to get attention, and she didn't really mean it. But then it was as though every time she did it she tried to prove to us a little more that she did mean it."

Jane: "I was really upset the last time. Allison told me about it. She said Laurie's parents didn't even know. I looked at Laurie. She was wearing a long-sleeved shirt, but I could see the bandages sticking out near her wrists. I just looked away. I kept wondering whether someone ought to tell her parents, but Allison said that Laurie had sworn her to secrecy.

"I kept thinking of my sister's friend who had died. The whole school came to her funeral. I tried to imagine the whole school coming to Laurie's funeral, standing around looking very solemn. I could almost hear Laurie's voice, in her sarcastic way, saying, 'I guess she was right, folks.'"

Beth: "I remember that big party we had at my house, when we had lots of kids and no grownups. At that party Laurie tried to commit suicide on us. It scared the hell out of me, but I've never been so mad. I was just furious. She was putting us in a position where we were responsible. Here this girl is committing suicide, and there are no grownups in the house. We were all a little high on pot, and we wouldn't have been able to handle the situation if it had been very serious. I didn't feel I should say anything to her then, but I was really mad."

Jane: "I don't get mad at her. I don't feel sorry for her either. I just want to know why she has to do it."

Beth: "Fine. I can't get mad at her if she wants to commit suicide. But if she's going to have the rest of us involved in her suicide attempt, it's just not fair. If she had committed suicide that night, I would have felt guilty for the rest of my life for not being there at the exact right moment. It put us in an awful position. That's why I was mad."

Jane: "I wish I could understand why she does it. When I'm with her I try to talk to her about it. But if you ask her why, she'll never give you a real answer. Then a few days later she'll bring up something and expect you to understand. It's so hard with her."

Beth: "Well, she tells us some things. I think we can

cope better with her suicide attempts than most grownups could. But you can never get her to discuss things seriously."

Jane: "I think there's something in her that likes the meanness people give her. If someone is nice to her she questions it and does something to make them be mean to her again."

Beth: "I don't know if she likes meanness, but she does do things that get everybody mad at her. I mean, I try to talk to her about her feelings and why she makes these attempts, and she'll just change the subject, or laugh or start to draw something. Yet she goes and makes attempts —like that one at boarding school—when people are around. Why would you do it in a place like that if you didn't want people to stop you and notice you? But when she's gotten others involved and they try to talk to her about it, she won't give a straight answer.

"That's why people get angry at her suicide attempts. And half the anger is fear. You think of yourself, and it's out of your hands, and you get mad and you get scared, for her and for you."

What would you do if a friend made an attempt on her life while in your home? What would you do if someone you care about confided that she had slashed her wrists, but made you swear not to tell her parents? And what would you do if a person you felt close to constantly threatened suicide, but then refused to talk to you seriously about those threats?

Probably you would feel angry, confused, and frustrated, as Beth and Jane did. Like them, you might care enough about your friend to keep trying to help and be supportive. Or, like most other people, you might decide that your friend just wants attention, and the best thing to do is ignore her.

Suicidal people have a way of defeating themselves. More than anything, they want to reach out to others. Yet in everything they do they turn those they need most against them. They manipulate friends and relatives. They make other people feel guilty and responsible for their actions, yet helpless to change things. And eventually the others begin to pull away, to free themselves from the burdens being imposed on them. Most suicidal people dislike themselves, and they make people they know dislike them too. They seem to invite "meanness," as Laurie's friend thought she did. But all the while they feel frightened and lonely. And they desperately need help.

Friends, relatives, teachers, co-workers—the everyday people in a person's life—make up the front line of defense against suicide. They are the people who can give the most immediate help in a suicidal crisis. And they must help, even if they believe the suicidal person is manipulating them or using threats of suicide to gain attention. A person who must resort to suicide to get attention has lost the ability to communicate in normal ways. That person needs attention. Without it the next cry for help will be shriller, more desperate, more dangerous.

A suicidal crisis does not begin at the moment a girl slashes her wrists or a boy stuffs a handful of pills into his mouth. It begins when feelings of hopelessness and helplessness become overwhelming, when a person comes to feel that he or she can no longer go on living as before. The crisis builds toward the suicidal act, sometimes gradually, often rapidly. Whether that act takes place at all may depend on how quickly others intervene to stop it, how attentively others pick up the messages and clues that suicidal people send out. If you suspect that someone you know is thinking

84

about suicide, watch the person; listen for messages; look for clues to suicide.]

1 Has some event plunged the person into deep depression and feelings of worthlessness—the loss of a parent, the breakup of a romance? Or is the person beginning to recover from a severe depression?

2 Is the person unusually withdrawn and uncommunicative, becoming increasingly isolated from others?

3 Does he or she seem preoccupied with thoughts of death, making blatant statements such as "I have nothing to live for," or probing more subtly into the value and meaning of life?

4 Have suicidal threats been made?

5 Did the person ever attempt suicide before, making another attempt likely?

6 Has the person suddenly gone on wild binges of drinking, taking dope, or carrying out other self-destructive acts that reveal a push toward death?

7 Has she or he suddenly become disruptive or violent in dealing with others, possibly masking suicidal thoughts behind angry actions?

X Does the person act peculiarly or irrationally, showing signs of severe mental illness that may lead to suicide?

8 Has there been some change in manner, some air of giving up that you can't quite pin down, but that makes you think, "Something is terribly wrong"?

Trust your own judgment. If you decide that a friend or relative may be in danger of suicide, act on your decision. As quickly as you can, tell others about your suspicions. Speak to the person's parents, friends, teachers, minister—key people in the person's life whom you think should be involved and can help. Diffuse the responsibility, and have others share with you, or take on themselves, the decision about what to do.

And don't be put off if others try to play down your

perception of how serious a situation is. Many people, including professionals in the health fields, miss suicidal clues. It's a sad fact that about 75 percent of the people who commit suicide visit a physician within a month or two before their deaths, and in most cases the physician either does not pick up warning signals or simply ignores them. If you fear that a friend or relative is becoming suicidal, insist that others pay attention. The worst you can do is be wrong, and feel foolish for stirring up a suicide scare where none exists. But you do far better to err in the direction of overcaution than to ignore the signals and take a chance on losing a life.

Telling others about a friend's suicidal plans or actions may mean making a painful decision to break a confidence. A boy may whisper that he has loaded his father's gun and plans to use it on himself. Or a girl may confide, as Laurie did to her friends, that she slashed her wrists and bandaged them, but her parents know nothing about the event. You swear to keep the secret. And you find yourself in the untenable position of feeling responsible for your friend, yet not knowing what to do to help. If you break the confidence and tell others, you will enrage your friend and probably lose the friendship. But if you keep the information to yourself and your friend attempts or completes suicide, you will feel guilty and responsible for years to come.

Keep this in mind. Your first responsibility in any suicidal situation is to preserve life, not friendship. The secret you have been asked to keep is not an ordinary one. And the confidence itself may have been a disguised message or plea for help. Laurie's friends followed her expressed wishes, and did not tell her parents about her wrist-slashing attempt. But then Laurie went on to make more blatant suicide attempts, aimed at her parents and designed to arouse their attention. Remember too that you are not in a position to judge how lethal or how genuine a person's suicide thoughts may be. You must take the information given you at face value, and pass it on to others in the hope that you can head off a suicide attempt.

Until others become involved, and even after they do, you can help ease a suicidal crisis by the things you say and do. Emotionally upset people sometimes play cat-and-mouse games in which they expect others to guess what they have on their minds through innuendoes of speech or sly glances fraught with meaning. It's not easy to get such a person to be open and honest with you. But you can encourage people to talk about their troubles by showing that you respect them and recognize the seriousness of their problems.

Don't try to reassure someone who feels deeply despairing that "there's nothing to worry about." A problem that you may consider trivial may appear intolerable to someone who is confused and depressed. "I understand how boxed in you feel, Harry," is a far more meaningful response to a friend's suicidal talk than, "Things can't be that bad, Harry, you're just exaggerating again." By showing that you sympathize and do not challenge your friend's sincerity, you make him feel comfortable about revealing troubling emotions and thoughts to you. While avoiding pat assurances, however, you need not give in yourself to a friend's feelings of hopelessness. You can point out that situations do change, and a problem that seems insurmountable one day may be solved on another.

Listen intelligently to what a disturbed person says to you, and try to reflect back to the person what he or she may be thinking. If a boy tells you that he would be doing his parents a favor by killing himself, you do not help him by insisting that such thinking is silly or "in your mind." You can help by reflecting his feelings back to him, and expanding on his thoughts, as in "I know you often think your folks don't love you, and I guess it's hard to love yourself when you feel that way." By bringing implied feelings out into the open, you help the boy clarify his thinking, and gain perspective on his situation.

Hard as it may be, you need, too, to speak frankly about a person's suicidal wishes. Most people would shy away from even mentioning the word "suicide" to a despondent person for fear of "putting thoughts into" the person's head. Such fears are nonsense. A girl who has been dwelling on visions of dying does not need to have thoughts of suicide "put into her head." The thoughts exist, even if she doesn't speak about them. When you confront them openly, you de-charge them, in a way, making it easier for her to deal with them directly. Such specific questions as "How long have you thought about killing yourself?" or "Were you thinking of using pills?" tell a suicidal person that messages and signals have reached their mark, and that you're concerned about what you've heard. The answers to these questions may also give you a clue to how serious the situation is. Generally, the more specific a person's plans, the greater the danger of actual suicide.

If you believe a friend or relative faces imminent danger of suicide, stay with that person until you can get other help, or until the immediate crisis passes. You may have to cancel all other plans to keep vigil during the crisis. You may infuriate the suicidal person, who yells at you to "leave me alone!" And you may feel stupid if you are wrong in your interpretation of the situation. But if you are right, you may save a life by being present at the moment when somebody needs you most. Nobody remains suicidal all the time. A crisis builds, and with the aid of others it may taper off. When you go out of your way to answer an urgent cry, you make the troubled person feel important and wanted. You help push the pendulum toward life.

* * *

Like friends and acquaintances, parents and family members who have picked up suicidal clues or have been warned by others of a person's suicidal intentions need to act quickly and decisively. If parents fear a suicidal act they should clear their home of all possible lethal weapons—guns, razor blades, ropes, or poisons in the form of household cleaners, medicines, sleeping pills, and other narcotics. They should not leave the young person alone in the house even if being home themselves means canceling work commitments and social appointments, and even if the suicidal person becomes furious at their precautions. They should try to speak to the person and to listen intelligently in order to understand, if they can, the causes for the crisis. And they should be in touch with friends, teachers, or school officials to get their view of the situation.

Almost always, too, parents of a suicidal boy or girl should seek professional help for that person. During a suicidal crisis, and even after the crisis has passed, a trained outsider should be called in to evaluate the situation and, if necessary, to work with the person and the family. The trained outsider might be a psychiatrist, psychologist, social worker, family counselor, or physician. Most important, the person should have experience in treating young people and dealing with suicidal problems. A therapist who has never worked on suicidal cases may feel threatened and overwhelmed by the problems posed, and be incapable of working effectively with the troubled person. The therapist should also be someone whom the patient and family can trust, and with whom they feel comfortable. Counseling or therapy for a young person usually involves the family in some way. No progress for the patient can be made if family members feel antagonistic or have no faith in the therapist's ability.

One good way to find a therapist or counselor is to

call a suicide prevention center, explain the situation, and ask for information and advice (the names and phone numbers of centers throughout the United States are listed in Appendix B). A community mental health center, the emergency room or psychiatric division of a local hospital, a student health service at a college or university, and various family service organizations in a community also can refer a suicidal person to a therapist or offer recommendations about how to proceed. A family physician or clergyman may be another useful source of referral and counsel.

A person who feels depressed and upset may welcome the opportunity to talk to a specialist who can understand and help without becoming emotionally involved the way parents do. And the knowledge that others care about them and have responded to their pleas helps many disturbed people pull themselves back from the brink of suicide. Even an acutely suicidal person may, with little opposition, accept the idea of being hospitalized as a protection against frightening self-destructive feelings.

But many suicidal people vehemently deny that they need help, and refuse to accept any. Convincing them to meet with a therapist or enter a psychiatric hospital becomes a sticky and draining problem. Sometimes, if all members of the family join together and exert strong pressure on the disturbed person, they can make some inroads. And sometimes a group of friends or a roommate or a favorite teacher can succeed far better than parents in pushing the person into therapy. In the most extreme cases, when severe suicidal danger exists, the person may have to be forcibly hospitalized by parents together with recognized physicians.

Nobody considers involuntary hospitalization an ideal solution to suicidal problems, and most psychiatrists avoid such a drastic step unless they believe it absolutely essential to save a life. A few psychiatrists insist that hospitalizing people against their will violates their civil rights, and should never be done. Most people in the mental health fields maintain, however, that in some crisis situations people must be forcibly hospitalized to protect themselves and to protect others. Even for a few days, hospitalization provides a cooling-off period that gives disturbed people a chance to pull their resources together, clear their minds, and get through the worst of their self-destructive feelings.

A therapist has one immediate goal in treating a suicidal young person, whether the person has entered therapy willingly or by force. That is, to make the person feel that others care. Underneath the hopelessness and despair of most suicidal people lies a devastating sense of worthlessness. Before they can cope with the causes that led to their unhappiness, they must be able to see themselves as worthwhile human beings whose lives deserve to be saved.

Once a patient has regained some self-confidence, he or she may begin more intensive psychotherapy. The patient may meet with the therapist one or two times a week, or more often if necessary. Together they explore the conflicts in the patient's life and the ways the patient has coped with those conflicts over the years. The process can be a painful and painstaking one, and the patient may become despondent again and again. But gradually the patient gains insight into his or her motives and feelings, and learns to solve problems without having to run away from life.

Unfortunately, for many young people, signals for help go unanswered until a crisis reaches the point of an actual suicide attempt. Then the person who survives a serious attempt is rushed to a hospital—not to the psychiatric division, but to the emergency room, where doctors and nurses direct all their efforts to saving the person's life.

A patient who awakens in a hospital after a suicide

attempt may deny that he or she ever made the attempt. "It was just an accident," the patient asserts, and holds firmly to that story in spite of all efforts to discuss the realities of the event. Or the patient may be furious at having "failed at even this," and secretly vow to complete suicide at the next attempt. A small number of patients experience a great sense of relief at being alive. For them the suicide attempt can become a turning point, and with the help of others, the beginning of a new life.

No matter what the attitude, a young person who has attempted suicide needs to be seen, evaluated, and usually treated by a professional therapist. And the reponsibility for seeing that the person gets proper treatment rests with parents and relatives. They cannot rely on the emergency room staff of a hospital to refer a suicidal patient for psychiatric care. Sometimes the staff will call in a hospital psychiatrist or psychologist for consultation on a patient who has attempted suicide. Then, after recovering from the attempt the patient may be transferred to a psychiatric ward. Often, however, emergency room staff members are too busy or uninterested to "bother" with psychiatric consultations. They "patch up" a boy or girl who attempted suicide, and send the person home.

How successful therapy will be after a suicide attempt or as a result of a suicidal crisis depends greatly on what kind of support the patient gets from family and friends. No suicidal child grew up in a vacuum, and no young person in treatment returns to a vacuum-sealed world. The lives of young people are intertwined with those of their parents, whether the parents are loving and supportive or rejecting and neglectful, and are influenced too by other relatives and friends. For this reason, therapists who treat young people try to involve parents, brothers and sisters, and occasionally close friends in the therapeutic process.

Sometimes a therapist who treats a suicidal person refers the parents to another therapist for treatment. And sometimes the same therapist treats both the parents and child, meeting independently with each, and occasionally holding joint meetings. Therapy for parents aims at helping them understand the kinds of pressures and problems that led to a suicidal crisis in their family, even if they themselves were not directly responsible, and teaching them to prevent future crises. The therapist also tries to show parents how to open channels of communication in the family so that young people can talk about their worries and unhappiness without having to use suicidal acts as their means of communication.

In the case of Laurie K., the support and care of friends and teachers along with intensive therapy for the patient and parents successfully prevented suicide and opened the way to a happier life.

Laurie began therapy with Dr. M. after she slashed her wrists at boarding school and was returned home. A sullen, angry, and profoundly unhappy sixteen-year-old, she agreed to see the psychiatrist only because she could no longer resist the urgings of her parents, friends, and teachers.

The "baby" in her family, Laurie was twelve years younger than her sister and ten years younger than her brother. Her birth, as she quickly pointed out to her therapist, had been an "accident." Her brother and sister had left home for schools and jobs while she was still a young child. And her parents, both highly successful lawyers, had immersed themselves in their careers.

Even as an infant, Laurie felt unwanted and unloved. A somewhat sickly and sensitive baby, she irritated her parents with demands and cries for attention. They returned her cries with lavish toys and gifts, but little of themselves. She came to see herself as an object that stood in everybody's way. But the more lonely and neglected she felt, the more demanding she became. And the demands, in turn, led to greater rejection by her family.

By her early teens, Laurie's life had become organized around a cycle of destruction. Because she had learned to dislike herself she needed to punish herself. This she did by provoking her parents into fierce anger at her. Their anger suitably reinforced her image of herself as worthless and bad, leading her to an ever greater need for punishment. That need she filled by slashing her wrists and becoming ill on overdoses of sleeping pills. In satisfying the drive to punish herself through these suicide attempts, Laurie also began to see self-inflicted death as a real alternative to an unhappy life.

During her early sessions with Dr. M., Laurie acted distant and guarded, convinced that he, like her parents, would view her as a worthless human being. The psychiatrist used various techniques to show his interest and concern for her. Sometimes during their therapeutic hour, the two left the office and took long walks together, talking all the way about her problems. Sometimes Laurie brought her best friends Beth and Jane to the office and as a group they discussed her actions and their reactions to her. At times during these sessions Laurie just listened quietly to what her friends said, and later reviewed their words and her feelings about them with Dr. M. When, at one of these sessions, Jane talked about Laurie's need to have people be mean to her, the words struck a responsive chord in Laurie. In later therapy sessions she returned again and again to her friend's comments, amazed that everyone but she had recognized her wish to punish herself.

With Laurie's permission Dr. M. also met with some of her teachers, and held several private sessions with

Ms. B., a drama instructor whom Laurie had made her confidante. The doctor and the teacher discussed ways of helping the girl and of handling her suicide attempts. At one of their meetings Ms. B. talked about her changing attitudes to Laurie:

"Laurie used to write about some of her attempts and her feelings in a journal that she kept and showed me. I saw that she had a great desire for me to be involved in or somehow present at her suicidal acts. Again and again in the journal it would say, 'I wish I could kill myself and my wrists would be bloody and Phyllis B. would be there to see it.' It really frightened me to recognize my importance to Laurie's suicide attempts.

"Recently, since we've been discussing all this, I've become much less frightened of Laurie and her capacity to die and drag me in there with her. I don't identify with her so much, and I don't feel so guilty either. I've become more conscious of what I say to Laurie and I've gained more control over the situation. I think I can really help her now."

During the course of Laurie's therapy, Dr. M. spoke often with her parents. At his suggestion they began therapy with a different psychiatrist, to work out their own complex problems of relating to one another and their children. From time to time the couple met with Dr. M. to talk about Laurie. Together they explored their own resentment of Laurie and their constant rejection of her. They recognized that they had always treated this child of later life as a burden to them. And as children do, she had taken the blame for being a burden onto herself, hating herself, as she believed others hated her.

Therapy for Laurie and her parents continued for several years. They did not change their attitudes easily. Nor did she give up her irritating and provocative behavior, or her suicide attempts, for a long while.

95

How You Can Help
in a Suicidal Crisis

Recognize the clues to suicide. Look for symptoms of deep depression and signs of hopelessness and helplessness. Listen for suicide threats and words of warning, such as "I wish I were dead," or "I have nothing to live for." Watch for despairing actions and signals of loneliness; notice whether the person becomes withdrawn and isolated from others. Be alert to suicidal thoughts as a depression lifts.

Trust your own judgment. If you believe someone is in danger of suicide, act on your beliefs. Don't let others mislead you into ignoring suicidal signals.

Tell others. As quickly as possible share your knowledge with parents, friends, teachers, or other people who might help in a suicidal crisis. Don't worry about breaking a confidence if someone reveals suicidal plans to you. You may have to betray a secret to save a life.

Stay with a suicidal person. Don't leave a suicidal person alone if you think there is immediate danger. Stay with the person until help arrives or a crisis passes.

Listen intelligently. Encourage a suicidal person to talk to you. Don't give false reassurances that "everything will be O.K." Listen and sympathize with what the person says.

Urge professional help. Put pressure on a suicidal person to seek help from a psychiatrist, psychologist, social worker, or other professional during a suicidal crisis or after a suicide attempt. Encourage the person to continue with therapy even when it becomes difficult.

Be supportive. Show the person that you care. Help the person feel worthwhile and wanted again.

Gradually, however, as Laurie began to see herself as a less worthless and more competent person, she gained new confidence in her abilities. Her schoolwork improved, and a latent talent for painting began to blossom. Her achievements pleased her parents, who could now take pride in her. And their pride and praises further encouraged her.

For Laurie the years of rejection, anger, and self-hatred might never be washed away completely. But with the cooperation of parents, friends and teachers she had much brightness and hope to look forward to.

7 Friends and Relatives

How Suicide Can Destroy
More Than One

"Just a few days before my friend killed himself he asked me how much tuinal could be fatal. He said he didn't want to go on anymore. I assumed this was just talk. You know, a temporary depression. When it became reality, it really shook me. I couldn't get over it. I still can't."—*high school junior*

"I'm not convinced it wasn't an accident. You know how careless he always was. I mean, if he really wanted to kill himself, he would have blown his brains out. I still think he was just cleaning his gun and it went off by mistake."—*father of a seventeen-year-old boy who had shot and killed himself*

"She didn't wake up with the joyous sense of facing a new day. She was sixteen, and she saw no excitement in the beginning of a day. Why didn't I realize how depressed she was?"—*mother of a sixteen-year-old girl who died of an overdose of sleeping pills*

"What a cruel thing for her to do. I don't think my

parents did anything to deserve that kind of cruelty and vindictiveness."—*sister of a fifteen-year-old girl who had slashed her wrists*

"She was worried she had cancer. Grandma—her mother—died of cancer and she kept thinking she would too. If only us kids had behaved better. Maybe if we wouldn't have fought with each other so much and made such a racket she wouldn't have been so nervous and worried all the time."—*twelve-year-old son of a woman who jumped to her death*

"I hope she knew how many people loved her and how much. I wish there had been some way to tell her and make it stick."—*author Erica Jong writing about poet Anne Sexton after her suicide*

These are the voices of the survivors, the parents, the children, and the friends who must go on living after somebody close has committed suicide. Some of the words printed above, such as Erica Jong's tribute to Anne Sexton in the *New York Times*, were circulated openly and widely. Most of the others were spoken softly in private conversations or written anonymously on the author's student questionnaire. All of them reflect the same feelings: hurt, guilt, shame, and anger.

During a suicidal crisis all the energies and abilities of family, friends, and professional people need to be mobilized to prevent the act of self-destruction. But once the tragedy of suicide takes place, the emphasis shifts. Now the survivors move to center stage and the suicide recedes into the background. Now the survivors become the victims, and sometimes, in their unending grief and sorrow, the potential suicides who must be cared for and saved.

No tragedy of life, no form of death arouses more

99

all-encompassing and inconsolable grief than does a suicide. No other kind of death turns those left behind so fiercely against themselves; no other kind leaves such lasting scars. A suicide in a family affects every member. Over the years, the lives of hundreds of thousands of young people and adults have been changed by the suicide of another person. Yet society offers little to ease the burden these people bear.

Suicide is an unmentionable, almost a dirty word in our society. It is an act that violates the most basic tenets of Western belief. Religions condemn it as a sin, and for years law books of many lands listed it as a crime. In early days courts punished families of suicides, and kings confiscated all the property of a man who took his own life.

Most of the old laws have disappeared, but society's cold condemnation continues. And with it comes shame and guilt for survivors. In a book about the suicide of his son Michael, journalist James A. Wechsler described how the police offered to hide the circumstance of the death, and a reporter volunteered to suppress the details if the family so wished. "Even in the numbness of those hours," wrote Wechsler, "we were astonished at the prevalence of the view that suicide was a dishonorable or at least disreputable matter, to be charitably covered up to protect Michael's good name and the sensibilities of the family."

This attitude of shamed secrecy is the cause for gross inaccuracies in suicide data. Whenever possible family and friends try to hide evidence of suicide from coroners and medical examiners who must determine the cause of death in questionable cases. They may discard suicide notes, or they may pressure officials with many kinds of "proofs" to show that the death was accidental. Out of sympathy for survivors, reporting officials frequently do list equivocal deaths as accidents unless they uncover clear-cut indications of suicide. Some coroners will report a death as suicide only if they find a suicide note. Since just a small percentage of people who commit suicide leave notes, many cases go unreported.

The view of suicide as something to be covered up and hidden from the world leads also to unnecessary suffering and isolation for the families of suicides. Friends and even relatives tend to keep their distance when a suicide has occurred. They tell themselves they don't know what to say or they don't want to bother the mourners. With these rationalizations they protect themselves from having to deal with the shame and self-accusations of the survivors.

Yet the period immediately after a suicide is the period when survivors most need help, from people who care about them and often too from professional therapists. They need to be able to talk about their tragedy with someone more objective and clear-headed than they possibly can be. They need to be able to wonder out loud what they did wrong, and to go over and over the details in an effort to make sense for themselves out of a senseless act. They suffer most when they must suffer alone, with their hurt and humiliation.

After any death of a loved person survivors go through what authorities call a "grief process." At the first news of the death those left behind feel shocked and disbelieving. "I can't believe he's gone," they tell one another, even if the person who died was old or sick and the death had been expected.

As the reality of a death sinks in, survivors suffer painful grief and sorrow. They may weep uncontrollably, lose their appetites, and have agonizing, sleepless nights. They feel angry, cheated, and bitter. Often they worry about the future, and wonder how they will be able to bear life without the person they have held so closely in love. Finally, often months after the death, survivors begin to function normally again. They make plans for themselves and focus their thoughts on the life ahead of them. This last stage is the healing stage in the grief process. The bereaved may experience sadness and a sense of loss for years to come, but they will be able to go on living, and usually to enjoy life.

The survivors of a suicide go through a grief process that also begins with shock and disbelief. But for them disbelief relates less to the fact of death than to the acceptance of suicide as the form of death. In almost every case of suicide relatives and friends insist at first that an accident caused the death. Even with clear-cut evidence of suicide, some never relent. They become enraged at officials who label the death a suicide, and sometimes blame others for their carelessness in causing the death. In one case, for example, the father of a teenage girl who had jumped to her death from the roof of a building loudly and persistently threatened to sue the owner of the building for his "negligence" in allowing the suicide to happen.

As survivors begin to accept the truth they turn their rage and resentment against the suicide. "How could she do such a stupid thing?" or "Why did he do this to us?" they cry out in anger and pain. And along with the anger comes guilt. They feel guilty for being angry at someone who is no longer alive, but more pressing, they feel guilty and blameworthy for the tragedy itself. "What the heck did I do wrong," sobbed the widow of a man who had killed himself, "and why was I such a nag, and what could I have done to be a better person?"

For many people affected by the suicide of another, grief doesn't resolve itself in healing and peace of mind the way it often does in other forms of death. The grief feeds on the anger and guilt and the never-to-be-answered question of "Why?" And it grows and spreads under the disapproval of society, leaving survivors dragged down by a depression that may never be closed off. Sometimes the depression leads to a cycle of suicide or self-destructive acts for the survivors themselves.

When a teenager or young adult commits suicide every aspect of the grief process becomes intensified for survivors. All those connected with the person—parents, brothers and sisters, friends—endure their own brand of suffering.

Parents feel most responsible. No matter how loving they had been to their child, no matter how many times they may tell themselves that drugs or mental illness lay at the base of the tragedy, they continue to blame themselves. "When we're alone in the house, Joe and I just sit and stare at each other, and think about Bob," said the mother of a teenager who had killed himself two years earlier. "We don't talk about it to each other, but I know we're both thinking the same thing: 'What did we do to make this happen?' "

Less obvious than parental suffering is the anguish of sisters or brothers of a young suicide. Every child has wished at some time of anger or jealousy for the death of an older or younger sibling. When such a death does occur, the child feels frightened and confused and somehow responsible. When the death results from suicide, the fear, confusion, and burden of responsibility may become unbearable. Many parents make the mistake of trying to hide the facts of a suicide from young children in a family. But the half-truths, the innuendoes, and the intensity of their parents' grief only add to the child's fears and desolation.

Older siblings of a suicide often feel torn between loyalty to their brother and sister and a passionate wish to make up to their parents for the hardship they have suffered. They feel angry at their dead sibling and angry at their parents, yet helpless and despairing because they were unable to ease the pain each caused the other.

"I hoped that somewhere above us in the smoke

circled the shade of my brother Peter, who had taken his life," wrote a college student describing his thoughts after his brother's funeral. "I hoped that he watched us . . . that he watched me begin to tear myself from him. I wanted him to gnash his teeth and drift out of all reckoning. I wanted to ruin him as he had ruined us. I wanted him to truly die if he had so chosen. I wanted so very very much to be glad."

Guilt and confused loyalties also plague friends of a young person who has committed suicide. Parents of the suicide often silently accuse the person's friends for not having reported their child's drinking, drug-taking, or talk of suicide. And the friends themselves wonder time and again what they could have done to prevent the death, and in what ways they might unwittingly have encouraged the tragedy.

Herb A., a college sophomore, blamed himself completely for the suicide of his roommate Leon. Herb appeared at his school's student health clinic one day, looking haggard, unshaven, and tearful.

"You've got to help me," he told staff members. "I think I'm going crazy. I have nightmares every night, and they're tearing me apart. I can't eat. I can't sleep. I can't study. I can't go on living.'

Herb's nightmares and the torments of his days all concerned his friend Leon. The boys had become roommates during their first year of college. Both were bright, happy, outgoing, and athletic young men, excited about being away from home and proud of their prestigious Ivy League school. They had a fine freshman year, and looked forward to rooming together through all their college years.

After summer vacation, however, Leon began to act strangely. He complained of constant headaches, dizziness, and double vision. Urged by Herb, he had himself examined at the college infirmary, where doctors discovered a brain tumor. Surgeons at the community

104

hospital found the tumor to be malignant and inoperable. The prognosis: hopeless.

Leon decided to stay in school and continue as long as he could. Although shocked and frightened by the tragic news, Herb cheered his decision, and vowed to remain at his side to help him. The sick boy deteriorated rapidly. He became skinny and wan, spoke in slurred tones, and had trouble coordinating his arms and legs. At night he tossed and turned in pain, or awakened with severe convulsions.

Herb watched the slow death of his friend with horror and helplessness. He found himself increasingly trying to escape Leon's presence, spending his days in the library and his nights with other friends. He lost a great deal of weight, and had difficulty concentrating on schoolwork. But he adamantly resisted pressures from his parents and friends to move out or find a different rooming arrangement for Leon.

As time went on, Leon became despondent. Sick from his illness, he also felt isolated and rejected. Several times he spoke of taking his life to end his misery. Each time Herb encouraged him to keep fighting, but the encouragement was half-hearted. One evening, while Herb slept in another friend's room, Leon swallowed all the medications he had. Herb found his body in the morning, and had the task of notifying school authorities and the dead boy's parents. For weeks afterward, Herb lay awake nights in the room he had once shared with Leon, trembling with fear and crying uncontrollably.

The staff psychiatrist at the student health service met with Herb for several consultation sessions. They talked about Leon's death and Herb's feelings throughout the long illness. Herb came to understand that beneath his loyalty and sympathy for Leon lay a wish— a very natural wish—for Leon to die and thus end an existence that tortured both him and others. When

Leon's suicide fulfilled Herb's unspoken desire for his death, Herb became overwhelmed with guilt and self-blame. Facing his feelings and dealing honestly with his guilt gave Herb the strength and will to resume his normal life.

As a result of Herb's treatment, the clinic staff held a series of group meetings with Leon's classmates and teachers. All spoke of their sadness and guilt, their inability to aid Leon while he lived or to prevent his lonely death. Recognizing those feelings and talking about them helped all the people affected by Leon's suicide to cope with it.

Of all the survivors of a suicide, perhaps those most damaged by it are children who survive the suicide of a parent. "Sons of suicides seldom do well," wrote Kurt Vonnegut, Jr., in *God Bless You, Mr. Rosewater*. Nor, he might have added, do daughters. Children of suicides have a higher than average rate of suicide, not because the tendency toward suicide is biologically inherited but because they grow up with a heritage of guilt, anger, and a sense of worthlessness.

"Survivor guilt" is a major factor in the suffering of a young person after the suicide of a parent, according to psychiatrist Robert Jay Lifton. All children go through "little survivals" throughout their growing years, says Dr. Lifton. Each painful separation from a parent, each withdrawal of love or threat of rejection—what Dr. Lifton calls a "death equivalent"—that a child experiences leaves in its wake feelings of guilt and blame. The guilt becomes compounded in a child whose parent commits suicide. The child wonders, "What did I do to make my mother kill herself?" or "Why did my father die while I stayed alive?" And these thoughts, added to the existing storehouse of guilt and self-doubt, put this child in a far more dangerous and self-destructive position than an ordinary child.

For some young people the incessant guilt leads to attempts to "atone" for their feelings by their own suicide or self-destructive acts. On a more mystical level, children of suicides sometimes kill themselves in order to be reunited through death with the parent who abandoned them so abruptly.

A college student who was four years old when his father committed suicide described in chilling terms the special survivor guilt that remained with him through life:

"I still suck my thumb, and I hate death. The thumb stands for my weakness, my inability to overcome it. I am afraid of death . . . I was afraid, for years, to think of my father's death. I am afraid to think that the only relief from my guilt over his death can come from the ultimate psychological resolution of the desire to get back to him, to absolve myself in pure relation: to join him in death. I am afraid that what the Ouija board spelled out to me, that I would die when I was twenty-five, is true. I am afraid of my own power over myself, afraid of my father in me as death, afraid that guilt will seize my life. I hate death like I hate the father who won't let me use the force I need not to be afraid.

"I am afraid of aggression, I am afraid of what will happen if I lose control. Somewhere in my head aggressive thoughts killed my father; the will came from the desire to have my mother all to myself. His death scared me from any such will in the future; I am afraid of my mother's implicit challenge to step forward and take his place. So I suck my thumb, am a nice boy, passive. I wouldn't hurt anyone."

The boy's tortured thoughts and feelings are typical of the reactions of other young peeople to the tragedy of a parental suicide. But they do not have to be the only reactions. The emotions surrounding the survival and the struggle to give meaning to that sur-

107

vival may be turned into a creative force rather than a destructive one, Dr. Lifton suggests. Much depends on the attitude of the surviving parent, and the kind of care and nurturing the young person receives. If a survivor can enjoy loving relationships and a sense of vitality and affirmation in life, these forces may be able to overcome morbid thoughts and wishes for death, and serve as a wellspring for creative activity.

The love and nurturing that Dr. Lifton speaks of for young people are important for all survivors of suicide. Nobody can minimize the impact of a suicide. Nor can anybody free survivors of the anger, guilt, and pain they feel. But any one of us can help survivors do the "mourning work" necessary to go on living meaningful lives and save themselves and their families from further self-destruction.

From the moment a suicide occurs, survivors need the help and intervention of others. "Postvention" is the term psychologist Edwin S. Shneidman coined to describe this help. It means giving survivors the support they need just after a suicide and, over a period of time, helping them come to terms with the tragedy that has struck them.

What can you do to help a friend whose mother has committed suicide or a father whose son has killed himself? The most immediate thing is to encourage survivors to speak to a professional person whom they trust: a psychiatrist, psychologist, social worker, minister, rabbi, or physician; or, for a young person, a school psychologist, teacher, or administrator. These people can help pull them through the first stages of shock and disbelief, and then help them cope with the anger and guilt that come next.

Young people especially need to be encouraged to air their feelings rather than keep them locked within. The example of Herb A., who accused himself of the suicide of his friend Leon, applies to other young men and women as well. Herb's school had an enlightened student health service, attuned to the psychological needs of their patients. The kind of help they gave Herb and his friends is the kind of help many young people need after the shock of a suicide.

Many of the families in which suicides occur are disturbed families torn apart by problems and conflicts that may have contributed to the suicide. For them, long-term intensive therapy that includes all family members may be necessary. Other families may want to meet only periodically with a professional after the initial meetings. One important meeting time would be the first anniversary of a suicide, when old wounds may come apart and old emotions pour out and overwhelm survivors once again.

Aside from the help professionals can give, survivors of a suicide need the sympathetic understanding of friends and relatives. They need to be able to open their hearts to people who will neither judge them nor patronize them, but will simply listen intelligently. "Listening to someone else talk. How simple," says sociologist Samuel Wallace, "and how few do it." Wallace conducted in-depth interviews with twelve widows of suicides over a period of a year after their husbands' deaths. Throughout the investigation, interviewers listened and tape-recorded the widows' words, saying little themselves. At the end of the program the women agreed that being able to talk about their feelings had been an enormous help. "It saves your life, really," said one woman.

Listening to the survivor of a suicide, like listening to any person caught up in powerful emotions, involves responding to what the person says and feels. False reassurances don't work here any more than they do for a person teetering on the edge of self-destruction. You cannot undo the finality of a suicide. But you can point out to survivors that a suicide in a

109

family is not a shameful matter to be hidden away. It is a tragedy that destroys one life and disrupts many others. Dealing with it openly can help preserve those other lives.

Part Three:
Society
and Suicide

8 Underlying Causes

Who's to Blame?

The learned men took their seats as the chairman called the meeting to order. Some settled back to listen attentively to their colleagues. Others prepared pencils and paper to jot down notes.

The meeting had a special and somber purpose. It had been called to discuss an unexplainable outbreak of suicides among high school students, an outbreak so widespread that it had been labeled an epidemic. Why do young people on the threshold of life try to snuff out their existence, the men had been asked. Was the school system responsible?

The meeting quickly wandered from problems of high school students to the more universal question of why anybody commits suicide.

"Suicide is a childish form of reaction . . . ," one speaker said. "Like neurosis and psychosis, it represents an antisocial escape from the injustices of life."

"Nobody commits suicide who has not given up hope for love," stated another speaker.

"Nobody kills himself whose death is not wished by another person," contributed one more scholar.

"No one kills himself unless he also wants to kill others," added yet another member of the group.

On and on the speakers went, each scholar presenting his ideas about suicide in terms that related to larger theories of human nature he had worked out over many years.

When all the speakers had finished, the best-known and most influential among them rose to address the group.

"I believe," he said, "that in spite of all the valuable material that has been brought before us in this discussion, we have not reached a decision on the problem that interests us. We are anxious, above all, to know how it becomes possible for the extraordinarily powerful life instinct to be overcome . . ."

That meeting took place more than sixty-five years ago, in 1910. It was held in Vienna, Austria, by members of the Vienna Psychoanalytical Society, which included the leading lights in the new and controversial field of psychoanalysis. Alfred Adler, Wilhelm Stekel, and the most famous and controversial of them all, Sigmund Freud, met with a prominent Viennese educator, David E. Oppenheim, to try to uncover the mysterious causes of suicide among Viennese high school students. It was Freud, the founder of psychoanalysis, who finally admitted that the meeting had accomplished little and that much more work in this area needed to be done.

Freud and his circle of psychoanalytic followers were not the first to try to answer the question of why people kill themselves. Since earliest days scholars, clerics, doctors, and ordinary men and women have grappled with the same problem. What makes some people try to end their lives, when so much in our tradition and culture motivates us toward living, when

114

society so despises suicides that their families suffer the stigma of shame and guilt, and when other people who have been subjected to the most grueling circumstances—tortured, degraded, deprived of hope—fight to keep every breath of life? And what leads young people who have "everything to live for" to give up everything and want to stop living?

Over the years dozens of theories of suicide written with thousands of words have been published. Some blame parents for the suicides of their children. Some blame society. Some blame heredity or body chemistry. Yet for all the scholarly weight behind each theory one thing stands out clearly: No single cause can explain all suicides. Suicide is such a complex matter that it involves every aspect of life, from the society in which a person lives to family background to psychological makeup and childhood history. All need to be considered in any attempt to unravel the mystery of suicide.

A good place to begin exploring the causes of young suicides is to find out how society influences suicide. More than seventy-five years ago the great French sociologist Émile Durkheim studied the relationship between society and suicide, and came to some conclusions that still apply today. Durkheim analyzed different kinds of suicides that grew out of different social conditions. He grouped suicides into three types and used special terms to describe each.

①"Egoistic suicide," according to Durkheim, comes about when a person feels alienated from society and has few binding ties. The suicide is a lonely, unmarried, and unemployed man may be thought of as an egoistic suicide. So may the suicide of a teenage girl who has run away from home and finds herself alone and friendless in a strange town.

②"Altruistic suicide" lies at the opposite pole. It oc-

115

curs among people so dedicated to a cause or to the values of their society that they put duty far ahead of their own needs. An example of altruistic suicides are the Japanese kamikaze pilots of World War II who crashed their planes into Allied warships, destroying themselves while they destroyed the ships.

③ "Anomic suicide," Durkheim's third category, occurs when a person experiences a sudden and great change in fortune or position in society. A rich man who kills himself after suddenly being forced into bankruptcy can be considered an anomic suicide in Durkheim's scheme of things. Durkheim used the term "anomic" also to describe entire societies in which social institutions have changed or broken down so quickly that people feel confused about their positions and goals. As you might expect, suicide rates in such societies are far higher than in more rigid ones in which each person knows his or her role in life.

We live in a society today that Durkheim would have classified as anomic, a society in which rapid changes have brought great unrest. The changes have had an especially strong impact on young people, and the mushrooming rate of young suicides reflects that impact.

Ways of life that people used to take for granted have changed radically in our society in just a short time. Where once the family served as a center for the teachings and traditions of society, today people question the very value of the family itself. Men and women experiment with alternate lifestyles unheard of in other periods. Single people who don't want to marry live together unmarried. Married couples who get bored with each other or with conventional married life experiment with "open" marriages and with new sex partners.

Even when traditional families have been established, separations and divorces have become so commonplace that marriages that last any length of time have become the exception. "Nowadays if your folks get a divorce," says one fifteen-year-old, "there's always somebody to talk to about it if you want to. All you have to do is go next door, and chances are your neighbors on one side or the other have been divorced."

Nearly one out of every two marriages ends in divorce in the United States, and about a million children a year are affected by those divorces. As a result of so many divorces, the number of single-parent families has risen to the point where one out of every six children is being brought up by only one parent—usually the mother. "Never in the history of any society have we had a situation in which only one person and sometimes less than one is left with the responsibility of bringing up a child," says social psychologist Urie Bronfenbrenner, who has made extensive studies of trends in American family life.

Along with the breakup of traditional family life, changing attitudes among women have sent scores of them out of their homes and into jobs, many because of financial pressures and others to build careers for themselves. More than half of American mothers with school-age children work outside their homes, and about a third of women with children under six hold jobs outside their homes. But society hasn't caught up with the new roles American women have been creating for themselves. Employment schedules rarely are flexible enough to allow working parents to be home with their children after school, and few adequate day-care programs exist to look out for young children whose mothers work. As a result, many children in low-income families, and in increasing numbers of middle-class families, are shunted about from relative to relative while mother works, or simply are left to fend for themselves.

117

All these shifting patterns of family life are a far cry from earlier times when mothers not only stayed home with their children, but family units included grandparents, parents, children, and other relatives all involved with one another and going about their business with a clear knowledge of what was expected of them. Much of family life in those days centered around religious beliefs and practices. Today, religion too has lost its hold on most people, but no other institution has risen to provide the support and stability it once offered.

On a broader scale, little in the overall quality of life today encourages the ebullient optimism and sense of progress that our ancestors had. We live in the shadow of nuclear war. Children grow up with the ominous knowledge that the world as we know it can be annihilated within seconds by the blast of a nuclear bomb. They also learn that our resources have become limited, that our environment has been despoiled and polluted as a result of years of callous and unthinking waste. Politically, wars, government scandals, and disillusionment with the country's leaders have made Americans cynical of government. Many young people scorn old forms of patriotism, but have found no new loyalties and commitments to substitute for them.

The changes that have taken place have happened in just a few decades, accelerating rapidly since World War II. Perhaps from the rubble of old institutions will grow new ones more suitable to a new and rapidly changing society. But for now, the changes have brought a feeling of anxiety and dislocation that hits young people the hardest.

Other forces add to the stresses of life for the young. In a society that measures success in terms of wealth and power, they feel great pressure to do well in school, get good jobs or enter the "right" professions, and to accumulate money and status. The "American Fairy-Tale" is the label psychiatrist Darold A. Treffert applies to the unreal expectations parents have of their children. For thousands of teenagers the fairy tale ends in drug addiction, alcoholism, mental illness, and suicide.

The American Fairy-Tale rests on a series of myths about happiness that parents hold. One of those myths is that "Happiness is things." Many adults so value material possessions that things have become a great deal more important to them than ideals or values. They see even their children as things that give their lives meaning and status rather than as real human beings with needs and desires of their own. Another myth in Dr. Treffert's fairy tale is that "Happiness is what you do, not what you are." This myth pushes the young into trying to achieve what their parents want—high grades or athletic standing—rather than develop their innate interests and talents.

Other myths of happiness include the beliefs that happiness results from having no problems at all rather than from learning to cope with problems, and that happiness comes from conformity. The conformity myth leads teachers and parents to expect each child to fit their own ideal image of what a child should be. "What happens," says one teenager, "is that before you're born God sorts your soul out. If you've got a round soul, he puts you on a round planet; if you've got an oval soul, he puts you on an oval planet . . . In my case God made a mistake. I've got an oval soul, and he put me on a round planet. The school keeps trying to file my soul round, like everyone else."

The pressures that make up the American Fairy-Tale have contributed to the rise in suicides among the young, and especially to spiraling suicide rates among college students. Suicide is the second cause of death for college students, and the rate of suicide among them is higher than it is for other young men and women of the same ages. Although pressure to achieve high grades and success is not the only factor leading to college suicides, it is an important one. Suicidal college students interviewed by psychologists spoke about their inability to discuss frustrations or failures with their parents. So imbued were the parents with their own fantasies of success and achievement for their children that they simply did not want to hear about the fears or self-doubts the students had. Many of the suicidal students worried constantly about doing well in school. No matter how high their grade averages, they always felt insecure, convinced that the next test or the next term paper would show them up to be phonies and academic frauds.

The stresses society places on the young affect some groups of young people in special ways. Two groups in which suicidal acts loom large are young black men and adolescent girls, black and white.

Black men in their early twenties have the highest suicide rate of any black people at any age. This pattern of black suicide contrasts sharply with that of whites, where, in spite of dramatic increases in young suicides, more older people than young ones kill themselves. In New York City about twice as many young black men as young white men kill themselves, and similar trends have appeared in other large urban centers.

What causes so many young black suicides? Rage, self-hatred and the frustrations of ghetto living, says Herbert Hendin in *Black Suicide*. Black children reared in big city ghettos often live in homes without fathers and in which mothers are away at work much of the time. Sometimes neighbors or relatives care for the children, and sometimes they care for themselves. As a result of their disturbed family life, many black children grow up filled with rage and a sense of hopelessness about ever getting the love and support they long for. For boys, who have no father with whom to identify, that despair may be even more intense than it is for girls. As they reach their teens and early twenties, their anger and hopelessness are compounded by the frustrations of ghetto life. Locked in by the poverty and ghetto culture in which they grew up, they are unable to achieve economic security and success in society at large. With a despairing sense that they will never find satisfaction in life, they kill themselves while they are young.

The rates at which young blacks kill themselves might be even higher than known if some kinds of murders were included among them, according to psychologist Richard Seiden. In these murders, called "victim-precipitated" murders, the victims seem to provoke others into killing them, often wielding guns or taunting others with threats of violence. Many black men look down on suicide as a weak and "feminine" way out of problems, defining masculinity in terms of physical strength and toughness. Rather than give in to "cowardly" suicidal wishes, these young blacks create violence around them, hurting others and at the same time getting themselves killed; dying, in their view, as heroes.

The changing patterns of suicides among young women in their teens and early twenties is also complex. Traditionally girls have been considered the major suicide attempters in society, performing many more suicidal acts that do not end in death than boys. In the population as a whole about three times as many women as men have usually attempted suicide in the course of a year, and about three times as many men as women have completed suicide. Some researchers estimate that, among young people, as many as nine times more girls than boys attempt suicide without completing it.

121

However, in some large cities, the ratio of completed suicides for young men and women narrowed during the 1970s, with many more girls and young women actually committing suicide than in the past. In California, the highest increase in suicide rates among any group of women in 1970 was among urban black women in their early twenties.

What is the significance of all this? Nobody has done intensive research to determine why so many young women express their dissatisfaction with life by making suicide gestures and attempts. It would seem logical to connect the large numbers of suicidal acts girls perform to their upbringing in our culture. Traditionally girls have been taught to be passive, unaggressive, and accepting of their roles as the "gentler" sex. And they have learned to get what they want in indirect ways, by being cute and charming rather than by asserting themselves openly and demanding things. When they are deeply unhappy they apply these long-ingrained teachings to their actions. They make suicide attempts—some dangerous, others less so—in order to be noticed or loved or taken seriously. They use roundabout ways to influence others and get the attention they crave, even at the risk of their own lives.

On the other hand, girls in our culture are also permitted to show emotions more readily than boys. It's acceptable for a girl to cry or scream or act "hysterical," whereas a boy who behaves that way is laughed at and considered weak and cowardly. Girls, therefore, tend to become more openly depressed, and to express their depression through suicide attempts. Raised to hide their feelings, boys act out those feelings, often violently and impulsively, in ways that fit their masculine images of themselves. As a result they make fewer suicide attempts, but those they do make are usually more violent, and more often fatal than the girls' attempts.

The apparent increase in completed suicides among young women in urban areas may reflect a growing aggressiveness and violence on the part of women, as some authorities have suggested. But other more complicated and more subtle influences seem to be at work in this situation. As women have tried to change their roles and raise their aspirations, they have met increasing frustrations and pressures. Young women about to enter the job market or undertake professional careers still find many doors closed to them. This is especially true of young black women, whose suicide rates, like those of urban black men, have risen sharply. Teenagers and young women who want to take on new roles also find themselves faced with intense competition for which their upbringing has not prepared them, and under great pressure to succeed and prove themselves competent. When the frustrations and stresses become too grueling, some choose suicide as their alternative to life.

Suicide involves so many variables that no simple or definitive answers exist to how patterns change or why they differ among the sexes. Sex differences in suicidal behavior is an area that calls for much more research by experts than has been done so far.

Social theories explain a great deal about the stresses and tensions that may lead to young suicides. But they do not, and cannot, explain why some young people take the drastic step of killing themselves while others manage to cope with the same pressing social conditions and live normal lives. Psychological theories, rather than sociological ones, offer insights along these lines. And many of those theories began with Sigmund Freud.

After the meeting of the Vienna Psychoanalytical Society in 1910 Freud began to delve seriously into the psychological causes of suicide. Although he never published a book or even a pamphlet on the subject, his ideas about it are spread through many of his most important works. One of those ideas, which has become a cornerstone of psychoanalytic theory about suicide, is the view of suicide as a form of aggression turned inward, against oneself. According to this theory, people who kill themselves actually are killing the image of a hated parent within them.

All children, said Freud, grow up with mixed feelings of love and hate for their parents. The feelings are mixed because the parents both give them the love and security they need and, at the same time, "civilize" them and compel them to hold back their own desires. Children identify themselves with these beloved-hated parents, and, in many ways, incorporate the image of their parents within themselves. You can relate this theory to everyday life if you think about how many times during the course of a day or several days you say things that sound just like your mother, or make a decision that you know is exactly what your father would have done.

As some children grow to adolescence and then adulthood, they develop fierce anger at this inner image of one or the other parent. Usually the anger stems from some deep hurt or loss suffered as a child; perhaps the parent died suddenly, but nobody helped the child handle the death, or perhaps the parent abandoned the child or treated the child badly. Because years of learning and habit have taught people that they may not harm their parents, when the rage and despair become overwhelming, these angry people try to kill the parent image within them by killing or hurting themselves. They also punish the real parent through the suffering their suicide causes.

To explain how it becomes possible for suicidal people actually to turn their rage and hatred inward and destroy themselves, Freud advanced the concept of a death instinct working within them. This instinct, according to Freud, exists in everybody. But in suicidal people it wins out over instincts for life and love that predominate in most people.

Although Freud's theory of aggression turned inward has been widely accepted and elaborated on by psychiatrists and psychoanalysts, especially in interpreting adolescent suicides, most specialists have rejected his ideas about instincts. One of his most ardent followers who did accept it, however, was Karl Menninger, who built his own theories of suicide on those of Freud.

Suicide, said Menninger, is a form of murder in which both the murderer and the murdered exist within one person. Every individual who attempts or completes suicide is driven consciously and unconsciously by three motives: the wish to kill, the wish to be killed, and the wish to die. The wish to kill grows out of the destructive parts of disturbed people, the parts eaten away by anger and hatred toward others. The wish to be killed that suicidal people experience stems from turning these angry and hateful feelings back against themselves, and wanting to punish themselves for having the feelings. And the wish to die comes from the workings of a powerful death instinct within suicidal people. Sometimes one or another of these drives takes over, influencing the outcome of a suicide attempt. For example, some people have powerful wishes to kill or be killed, but they do not really want to die. This contradiction in feelings may lead them to attempt suicide but not complete it, or to act in self-destructive ways that cause them pain and punishment rather than death.

Other writers and theoreticians who have tried to piece together the parts of the suicide puzzle have moved away from exclusively emphasizing aggression and rage to seeing how the attitudes suicidal people hold toward death influence their drive for self-destruction.

For some people, death becomes more real and more important than life itself. These people romanticize death, fantasize about it, and instill into it unreal powers that negate its actual meaning.

People who hold these views toward death usually suffer from deep depression, from what critic and author A. Alvarez describes as "terminal inner loneliness." A one-time suicide attempter himself, Alvarez explains in *The Savage God* that "by all the standards they have built for themselves" these people have found their lives empty and useless. Death to them represents both an escape from the emptiness and, in a distorted way, a new beginning. They become preoccupied with death, dreaming of it, lusting after it.

Poet Anne Sexton, who later died a suicide, described her feelings in "Wanting To Die":

Since you ask, most days I cannot remember.
I walk in my clothing, unmarked by that voyage.
Then the almost unnameable lust returns.

Even then I have nothing against life.
I know well the grass blades you mention,
the furniture you have placed under the sun.

But suicides have a special language.
Like carpenters they want to know
  which tools.
They never ask why *build.*

Most people like Anne Sexton who are obsessed with thoughts of death don't view suicide simply as a way to end life. For them the act of killing themselves takes on symbolic meaning. By choosing when and how they

126

will die they gain power and control. They master life by mastering death, and in that way they achieve a sense of immortality.

This romantic attitude toward death is an important force behind many young suicides. When young people contemplate suicide they often think of it as a long, peaceful sleep or interlude that will somehow make things better. Or they picture death as a way to punish others or to make others show love for them. And always, somewhere in their minds, is the belief that they will be present to benefit from the punishment their death has inflicted or the love it has aroused.

Lonely and unhappy young people, too, may build fantasies about death that give them deep satisfaction. Suicidal teenage girls sometimes picture death as a lover who will seduce them and carry them away. Young people who have lost a parent may dream of death as a way to be reunited with their loved one. Young lovers may make suicide pacts to immortalize their love through joint deaths. Such fantasies and dreams deny the one and only truth about death: that is, that it irrevocably ends life.

Theories that emphasize suicidal fantasies or angry wishes turned against oneself shed some light on the psychological makeup of people who take their own lives. But still something is missing. Why do some people become so involved in dreams of death that for them death seems more important than life? What causes such violent anger and aggression toward others that suicides must direct these feelings back to themselves?

The search for answers now shifts to another area of investigation: the influences family life and background have on shaping the kind of person we each become.

Whenever you get far enough along into social or psychological theories about young people, parents seem to come out as the heavies who must be blamed for everything that goes wrong with their children. This constant use of parents as scapegoats is unfair. Children are born with different temperaments and different personality factors, and their every action, good or bad, cannot be laid at the doorstep of their parents. In some cases nothing a parent ever did to a child can equal the suffering and pain with which the child "repays" the parent. In other cases parents are made to feel responsible and guilty for situations over which they have no control. Some mental illnesses, for example, are caused by chemical changes in the body or by brain damage. No matter how understanding and kind parents try to be, they cannot alter the symptoms or satisfy the sick person. If they arrange professional help for their child and cooperate in the treatment, they have done as much as they can do, and should not be held accountable for end results.

With that disclaimer, it must still be stated that parents' attitudes and the quality of family life have an enormous impact on the development of a child. More than anything else, family background and experiences during the early years of life play a major role in creating suicidal wishes among young people. Study after study has found that a large proportion of young suicide attempters and completers came from disturbed or disrupted homes, lacking in stability and support. In some disrupted homes parents were divorced or constantly quarreling; in others a parent had died or deserted the family, or one or another parent was an alcoholic or had spent considerable time in jail. Children who grew up in these broken homes felt abandoned and lonely, filled with anger at the parent who had hurt them and at themselves.

Psychologists often point to broken homes as the underlying cause for many kinds of antisocial behavior among young people, including juvenile delinquency, drug addiction, and alcoholism as well as suicide. The degree to which a child becomes depressed, isolated, and lonely within such an environment influences the extent to which that child becomes openly suicidal.

Depression, isolation, and loneliness, the precursors to suicide, do not, of course, plague children from broken homes only. And certainly every home that has suffered a death or a divorce does not produce suicidal children. The common denominator that may lead a child into depression and possible suicide in any home is a lack of love and support.

A child who grows up feeling unloved and unwanted becomes increasingly frustrated, angry, and depressed. Pathetically, the more children feel rejected and unloved by parents, the greater is their need for those parents, according to psychiatrist James M. Toolan who conducted a number of research studies on adolescent suicide. Because they cannot tolerate the thought that their parents really do not love them and never will love them, these children often twist reality so that they can blame themselves rather than their parents for their troubles. As children move toward the teen years, however, they find it harder to deny the truth of their situation. This is the time when they become enraged at their parents, yet so filled with guilt about their violent anger that they may turn the anger inward. And this is the time when suicidal thoughts grow, and fantasies about death nurture those thoughts. Almost anything can set off a suicide attempt at this time. Rejection by a girlfriend or boyfriend, an argument with a parent, or poor grades in school can stir up the buried, but ever present, feelings of being unloved and unwanted.

Parents can make a child feel unwanted in dozens of ways. In hostile and abusive homes, in which parents beat children or openly reject them, the message comes across clearly. Communication is more subtle, more insidious in many other homes. In these homes parents would never admit, even to themselves, that they did not want their children or that the children got in their way. But those feelings exist, sometimes consciously, more often unconsciously. And the children pick them up quickly.

Charlotte N. sensed her parents' feelings about her early in life, and had her intuitions confirmed after making a suicide attempt. Charlotte and her parents lived in one of the most exclusive suburbs of Boston, where Charlotte attended the finest schools. But for all their wealth and comfort, her parents were unhappy. Their life together revolved around a cycle of bitter arguments, separations, reconciliations, and then more arguments. Charlotte always figured in the arguments, with each parent accusing the other of not loving her and not devoting time to her.

At the end of her junior year in high school Charlotte joined a select group of students spending the summer in Paris, chaperoned by their French teacher. Soon after arriving at their Parisian hotel Charlotte made a suicide attempt by taking an overdose of sleeping pills her mother had given her "to calm her so she could sleep away from home." The teacher immediately called Charlotte's parents to urge them to fly to Paris and possibly take her home. Now in the midst of planning their "final" reconciliation, the parents made it clear to the chaperone that they did not want Charlotte home and underfoot.

"It takes Charlotte a while to adjust to new situations," said her father. "She had adjustment problems at summer camp, too, but then she settled in," he added, casually equating camp adjustment to a suicide attempt. Her mother's words were even more revealing.

"What a silly child," said this seemingly sophisticated woman, "I certainly hope I didn't give her any ideas. I sent along a bottle of my sleeping pills to help her get through the first nights away. I mentioned that a friend of mine had swallowed just about the same amount of pills all at once in a suicide attempt. Then I remembered something I had done at her age. I described how I had climbed a mountain not far from my home carrying a knife with which to end my life romantically because my boyfriend left me."

Charlotte would have been thick, indeed, to miss the hidden message behind her mother's suicide stories. If the message needed further clarification, it came when her parents decided not to visit her in Paris, but instead to let her "work things out for herself." They were going to London to celebrate their reconciliation. A week before Charlotte was due home, she slashed her wrist with a knife, barely missing an artery. Her parents' messages had hit their mark. As they came to take her home from a Parisian hospital, they began to realize that she too had a message to deliver.

"Growing up dead" is the way Herbert Hendin describes the lives of young people whose parents didn't want them and unconsciously wished them dead. In his study of suicidal college students he found that most of them grew up sensing that their parents felt most comfortable with a lifeless child who caused them no trouble. To please their parents they learned to have no feelings and make no demands, to literally deaden themselves emotionally.

When these young people went off to college they began to experience feelings of excitement and challenge for the first time. These new feelings thrilled them, but also terrified them because they threatened to disrupt the quiet nonexistence that had been the backbone of the students' lives. Many attempted suicide in order to continue, and carry to its logical con-

131

clusion, the deadness they knew their parents expected of them.

Who's to blame for the young suicides? A complexity of causes that involve social, psychological, and family interactions. Rapid changes in society have disrupted family life and created increasing numbers of disturbed or dissatisfied homes. In many of these homes children grow up feeling unwanted, even wished dead or nonexistent by their parents. Such feelings may lead to inner rage and depression, and a wish to escape life through death.

9 Differing Attitudes

Crime, Sin, or Right?

"I don't think suicide will solve any problems for you or your loved ones, because you will just cause sorrow and pain for others."

"If one feels utter disgust and despair with the human race and life in general, one has every right to kill one's self."

"Suicide is murder. There's always an alternative—living is one of them."

"If anything can be called a human right, suicide definitely is. To deny a person death is unjustifiable. I have never seriously considered suicide, but I always know the option exists—and this is a comfort."

"If you can't decide when and where you will be born, why should you have the right to take your life away?"

"Just as I want to make a conscious choice about bringing life into the world by intentional pregnancy, I want the choice of going from the world intentionally through suicide. Neither pregnancy nor death should be accidental, the result of thoughtlessness."

"In a broad sense suicide can never be justified in that it does not affect one person only. It can have disastrous effects on family and friends, and a person should never have the right to inflict that kind of pain."

"Death is an end. If something is unpleasant enough to warrant its end, then it should be ended."

"I can understand why some kids come to think life is no longer worth living, but I don't think they're right. American society allows one, in fact encourages one, to believe that life is wonderful. If it isn't that day, then go out and buy something that'll make it better. But life and happiness cannot be bought and sold. They take working at, perfecting."

These conflicting opinions about suicide come from the author's survey of high school and college students, in answer to the question "Do you think suicide among young people is ever justified?" Almost half the students (49 percent) answered "Yes," and supported their view with strong arguments. More than a third (38 percent) answered "No," and used equally forceful arguments to back their opinion. A small number of students had no opinion, or answered that they could not make up their minds.

Questions about the justification of suicide and the "right to die" have become hotly debated in our society. For the first time in history medical science has been able to prolong life beyond its natural course. Heart resuscitators, kidney machines, breathing devices, drugs, and other artificial mechanisms keep life going for people who might otherwise die. These medical advances have brought renewed life and hope to thousands of people. But to others they have brought a meaningless vegetable-like existence. Patients may be labeled officially alive while they lie in a coma for months, sometimes years.

134

Or they may be bound to beds, immobile, barely functioning.

And the questions have arisen: Should terminally ill people be allowed to choose death rather than life? Should physicians be permitted to "pull the plugs" on life-giving machines when the quality of life has become meaningless? From these questions have come even more difficult and threatening ones, extending to far broader areas. Should anyone who feels life has become meaningless have a right to end life? Are there times when society should not try to prevent suicide?

Although these questions relate specifically to our own society, every society in history has wrestled with similar ones. Each has had to determine when, if ever, suicide can be justified, and when, if ever, it should be permitted. Obviously no society can survive if it allows widespread suicide among its members. And in most cultures and most times in history people have feared, forbidden, and condemned suicide. But at certain times, and under certain conditions, they have not only tolerated but also encouraged it.

Early societies sometimes forced certain members into committing suicide for ritual purposes. Behind the ritual lay a powerful belief in life after death. On the Fiji Islands, for example, tribal peoples expected the many wives of a chieftain to kill themselves when he died. The women competed with one another in rushing to destroy themselves, with the belief that the first to die would become the chieftain's favorite wife in the world of the spirits.

Similar thinking and similar pressure from society motivated widows in ancient India who practiced suttee. These women threw themselves on their husbands' funeral pyres or drowned themselves in the Ganges River under the encouragement of Hindu priests and their own relatives. The priests taught that by killing herself a faithful wife could atone for her husband's sins on earth and open the gates of paradise to him. People venerated a woman who practiced suttee; they condemned one who refused, sometimes threatening her with severe punishment. This ancient practice continued in India for hundreds of years. Even after it was outlawed by British rulers of India in 1829, slow-changing customs kept it going in the 1900s.

In many early societies suicide or suicide-like activities served as a means to regain lost honor. Among some early African tribes, and well into modern times, men revenged themselves upon their enemies by committing suicide, a practice known as "killing oneself upon the head of another." When such a suicide took place, custom dictated that the enemy who caused it must immediately kill himself in the same way.

In North America, northern Cheyenne Indian warriors who had lost face or been shamed placed themselves in life-endangering situations. They might go on a buffalo hunt or organize a war party against a neighboring tribe or inflict pain on themselves in a dangerous ritual dance. If a warrior acted bravely and succeeded in his venture, he won great honor among his tribesmen, and regained his lost self-esteem. If he failed and died, the tribe considered his death an honorable one.

Ironically, lack of self-esteem without a traditional way of regaining it became a major cause for a high rate of actual suicides among Cheyenne Indians in modern times. Closed in on reservations, the Cheyenne lost their pride, many of their traditions, and their old means of supporting themselves. They became subservient to white people, and dependent on them for support and social welfare. With war parties, buffalo hunts, and other long-accepted methods of handling feelings of unworthiness and dishonor forbidden to them, many young men turned instead to open suicide.

The ancient Chinese regarded suicide as an acceptable way for a defeated general or a deposed ruler to regain honor. And the Japanese ritualized suicide in the form of hara-kiri as a ceremonial death with honor for samurai, or members of the military class. A samurai warrior might commit hara-kiri if he had humiliated himself or disgraced his family in some way. Or after his chief died he might kill himself to show allegiance to his leader. And sometimes an emperor would order a samurai warrior to commit hara-kiri to avoid the disgrace of a public execution. The ritual of hara-kiri involved a highly elaborate process of disembowelment that might take hours to complete. A second person ended the ritual by cutting off the suicide's head.

Although Japan outlawed hara-kiri in 1868, the tradition of suicide in the name of honor continued to influence Japanese practices. During World War II more than a thousand young Japanese soldiers died as kamikaze pilots who hurtled their planes against Allied warships. Shortly before Japan's defeat a number of army and navy officers commited ritual hara-kiri rather than accept surrender. More recently, in 1970, the famous Japanese author Yukio Mishima committed hara-kiri as a plea to his countrymen to return to old traditions and old values, of which one was the concept of dying with honor.

The old Japanese glorification of death with honor may be partly responsible for the exceedingly high rate of suicide among young Japanese today. More than twice as many Japanese young people as American between the ages of fifteen and twenty-four kill themselves. Deep feelings of insecurity that develop in many Japanese homes, along with fierce competition in school and in the job market, play an important part in these suicides, according to studies that have been made. But traditional attitudes to heroic suicides have also made other suicides more acceptable to the Japanese. Even the most

137

despairing young man, for example, can identify himself in some ways with the noblemen of old, and view his suicide, like theirs, as a way of gaining honor.

Unlike the Japanese and Chinese, Moslems have always strongly condemned suicide. The Koran, the holy scriptures of Islam, declared suicide to be a more serious crime than homicide. Behind this attitude lay the Moslem belief that each person has his or her Kismet, or destiny, which is foreordained by God and must not be defied. Although some suicides take place in Moslem countries, strong religious prohibtions have kept rates relatively low.

Judaism, too, regards suicide as a sin. Although the Old Testament did not specifically prohibit it, Jewish laws compiled after biblical times forbade it, and denied full religious burial rites to people who kill themselves. In spite of these prohibitions Jews through the ages have recognized and honored heroic suicides committed to avoid being murdered, forced into idol worship, sold into slavery, or sexually abused.

The ancient Hebrews became known for one of the most heroic and spectacular mass suicides in the ancient world. It happened in A.D. 73 at the fortress of Masada on the edge of the Judean desert overlooking the Dead Sea. The Romans had conquered Judea and destroyed the Second Temple in A.D. 70, but a garrison of about a thousand men, women, and children of the Zealot sect held the fortress and used guerrilla war tactics to resist Roman forces. When defeat seemed inevitable the Zealot leader Eleazar ben Jair urged his people to kill themselves rather than become Roman slaves. According to the Jewish historian Josephus the soldiers slew their wives and children. Then they drew lots to determine who among them should slay their companions and then destroy themselves. By the time the slaughter ended, some 960 persons had been killed or had taken their own lives. Two women and five children escaped the massacre and remained alive to tell the story recorded by Josephus.

The theme of dying with honor to preserve one's beliefs continued throughout Jewish history, as Jews suffered persecutions and tortures in different countries in which they lived. In some ways the closest parallel to Masada came during World War II in Treblinka, one of the most horrible of the Nazi concentration camps. Thousands of Jews from Eastern Europe were sent to this camp to be exterminated. Most lived the short time they had alive there in trance-like states, numbed to everyone and everything around them. Then one by one people began killing themselves, and their deaths served as an affirmation of their freedom to control their own lives and deaths. Their suicidal acts led also to the first signs of solidarity among them, with those who remained alive helping those who wanted to kill themselves so they would die quickly. These flickerings of friendship marked the beginning of a rebellion that later took the form of open revolt, one of the few such revolts that occurred in a concentration camp.

Ancient Greeks and Romans did not hold as clear-cut attitudes toward suicide as the Jews. Greek city-states differed greatly in their laws about suicide. In Thebes people condemned a person who committed suicide, and permitted that person no funeral rites. In Athens law courts decreed that the hand of a suicide must be cut off and buried apart from the rest of the body, because the hand had committed the evil deed. In other Greek communities, however, special tribunals existed to hear the arguments of people who wished to end their lives. If a magistrate thought a defendant had a convincing argument for suicide, he granted permission for the act to take place. Magistrates in some towns even provided would-be suicides with the poison hemlock with which to kill themselves. Generally magistrates considered insanity, profound physical suffering, or overwhelming sorrow as sufficient causes for suicide.

Roman law regarded suicide as a crime mostly when it hurt the government or economy of the state. The suicide of a soldier, for example, was especially condemned because it represented a loss of manpower to the army. On the other hand, the Romans had great respect and admiration for men and women who committed suicide to defend a cause or to honor their country. The statesman Cato the Younger received high praise because he killed himself rather than agree to live under the rule of Julius Caesar. Even Caesar extolled his heroism, declaring, "Cato, I grudge you your death, as you have grudged me the preservation of your life."

In the later days of the Roman Republic, the permissive attitude of Roman law toward suicide combined with pessimistic views of Roman philosophers encouraged a spate of suicides among noblemen and wealthy landowners. Each vied with the other in attempting to die with the greatest dignity, courage, and style.

Attitudes toward suicide changed radically after the Christian church became the dominant force in Europe during the Middle Ages. At first, early Christians who lived under Roman rule glorified suicides that were committed in the cause of martyrdom. Persecuted and despised, these early Christians looked forward to joys of immortality in another world. Many killed themselves or submitted willingly to Roman torture and execution. Others tormented themselves or led such ascetic lives that they died of hunger and illness. Their deeds created a kind of cult of martyrdom, joined by thousands.

But by the end of the fourth century St. Augustine laid down rules against suicide that became the basis for Christian doctrine throughout the ages. Arguing that suicide allows no opportunity for repentance, he branded

140

all suicides crimes. He even condemned the suicides of women who killed themselves to prevent rape, a motive that earlier Christians had highly respected. To justify the church's veneration of earlier martyrs, Augustine maintained that many of them had received revelations or guidance from God.

The teachings of St. Augustine and other early church fathers became incorporated into the laws of the Roman Catholic church and later the Anglican church. Church councils declared suicide to be an act inspired by the devil. They proclaimed it a mortal sin, and ruled that the bodies of suicides be denied Christian burial and that even attempted suicides be excommunicated. Church laws did distinguish between the suicides of sane and insane people, and also exempted young children from the penalties of the laws. These religious laws against suicide have remained in effect in the Roman Catholic church and in many Protestant churches, although priests and ministers have found ways to modify them in special circumstances.

As a result of the strict rules of the church and the power it wielded, suicides were rare during the hundreds of years of the Middle Ages. When a suicide did occur, townspeople degraded and mistreated the body. Sometimes they dragged it through the streets to be spat on or hung on public gallows. Sometimes they buried it on the spot where the person had died, and other times they left it unburied in the area reserved for public executions. Often a suicide's body was superstitiously buried at a crossroads with a stake through its heart and a stone on its face to prevent the spirit of the dead person from rising.

In England, as late as 1823, the body of a suicide named Griffiths was dragged through the streets of London and buried at a crossroads. Mr. Griffiths became the last suicide in England whose body was so desecrated. Parliament quickly passed a law ordering that the corpse of a suicide be buried privately in a churchyard or in a private burial ground. A law passed in 1961 repealed old civil rulings about suicide that had been based on Anglican church doctrine. Today neither suicide nor attempted suicide are treated as crimes in England.

American law, based on English law, was always more liberal in regard to suicide. Suicide has never been a crime in the United States, and the property of suicides has never been confiscated. Attempted suicide is regarded as a felony in only nine states—Alabama, Kentucky, New Jersey, North and South Carolina, North and South Dakota, Oklahoma, and Washington—but even there attempters have almost never been prosecuted. And states rarely prosecute people who help others attempt or commit suicide, although most state laws regard such help as a criminal offense. But the stigma against suicide that goes back to earliest times still remains.

While religious doctrines and civil laws about suicide developed and changed from society to society, philosophers and thinkers approached the problem of suicide from their own points of view, in terms of ethics and morals.

One of the most famous suicides of ancient times was that of the Greek philosopher Socrates, teacher of Plato. Socrates died by his own hand, drinking a cup of hemlock, but his death was really a form of execution ordered by the rulers of Athens. Plato quoted Socrates as saying before his death, "No man has the right to take his own life, but he must wait until God sends some necessity upon him, as he has now sent me."

Like Socrates, Plato and his student Aristotle both disapproved of suicide. Because Plato viewed people as the "chattels" of God, he argued that they did not have the right to destroy themselves. Aristotle stressed the

142

cowardliness of suicide, an act that he considered an affront to the state, similar in kind to that of a soldier deserting his post.

The Greek Stoic philosophers who came later took a much more lenient attitude toward suicide, which stemmed from their view of death as a release from the sufferings of life. Stoic philosophers emphasized reason and virtue as the basis for a good life. Suicide became, then, not a matter of right and wrong, but of choosing the most reasonable way to act in a given situation.

Legend says that Zeno, founder of the Stoic philosophy, committed suicide after breaking his toe. Ninety-eight years old at the time, he decided that God had sent his broken toe as a sign that he had lived long enough. Cleanthes, his successor, supposedly took his life too. Cleanthes had developed a boil on his gum, and was told by a doctor not to eat for two days to allow the boil to heal. But the philosopher continued to starve himself after the boil healed because he argued, once he had gone so far along the path to death, he might as well complete the act.

Begun in Greece, Stoic philosophy reached its height in Rome. One of the leading Roman Stoics, Seneca, summed up the viewpoint of the others toward suicide when he wrote, "If life please you, live. If not, you have a right to return whence you came." But Seneca and the other Stoics did not advocate suicide as an impulsive escape from everyday life. They were concerned mostly with living good and rational lives, unhindered by debilitating old age, crippling sickness, or political tyrannies. They advised people to think carefully about the pros and cons of suicide before taking their own lives, and to allow themselves to suffer before rashly killing themselves.

Christian dogma, which dominated the Middle Ages, left little opportunity for philosophic discussions of the rights and wrongs of suicide. But the Renaissance in the

143

1500s and 1600s brought new waves of thought on the subject.

In France essayist Michel de Montaigne broke with the Christian church in its attitude toward suicide. Montaigne considered suicide to be foolish but not immoral. And he tried to understand and explain the kinds of situations that might lead people to suicide.

In England poet and preacher John Donne took suicide out of the exclusive realm of religion and morality, and placed it in the domain of the individual—the act of a man or woman driven by personal motives. Donne, who became dean of prestigious St. Paul's Cathedral in London, wrote a defense of suicide when he was young in which he admitted that he had contemplated suicide himself. Because of his personal revelations he refused to have the book, *Biothanatos,* published. His son finally published it in 1644, thirteen years after Donne died.

About a hundred years later the great Scottish philosopher David Hume wrote a short essay, "On Suicide," that also was published after his death, but then quickly suppressed. The essay argues against the view of suicide as a crime. "The life of a man," says Hume, "is of no greater importance to the universe than that of an oyster." It follows, then, that a man who kills himself does not disrupt the larger order of the universe. He also "does no harm to society; he only ceases to do good which if it is an injury is of the lowest kind."

Other eighteenth-century philosophers echoed Hume's defense of suicide as an individual's moral right. Like him, these thinkers wanted to wipe away centuries of superstition and prejudice against suicides, and to liberalize church doctrine at least enough to prevent the abuses heaped on a suicide's body. Prominent among these reformers were the French philosophers Jean Jacques Rousseau and Voltaire.

In his novel *La Nouvelle Héloise* Rousseau empha

144

sized the natural right people have to end their lives as long as they cause no harm to others by doing so. He established one condition: people who have responsibilities to others should not commit suicide. Voltaire pointed out in his writings that wars and the murders that accompany them are far more harmful to society than the suicide of one individual.

In the midst of the liberal voices of English and French thinkers, Immanuel Kant of Germany expressed a dissenting point of view. Kant agreed with the major religions that suicide is morally wrong, but he arrived at his conclusions from a different course of reasoning. Life is sacred, said Kant, because it is part of nature. As such, each life has a place in the vast laws of nature, and each person has a duty to preserve his or her own life. To ignore this duty and end life is immoral. True morality consists in rising above personal feelings of despair, fulfilling one's duty, and continuing life in spite of adversity.

During Kant's lifetime, in the late 1700s, the romantic movement in literature and the arts came into full flower, and with it came a new idealization of suicide. Young people everywhere sobbed over Goethe's novel *The Sorrows of Young Werther,* about a young man who kills himself after being torn apart by uncontrollable passions. Men began to dress like Werther, speak like Werther, and dream of destroying themselves like Werther. To suffer for one's genius; to struggle for art; to die young, a hero mourned by the world—these were the ideals of the romantic generation. Rationalism, religion, or morality had little to do with this new attitude toward suicide. Far more to the point was the comment of French poet Alfred de Musset who, when he saw a lovely view in nature, exclaimed, "Ah! It would be a beautiful place in which to kill oneself."

The romanticization of suicide continued for years, and still continues. But as usual other currents grew

145

alongside it, bringing different philosophic attitudes toward suicide.

The German philosopher Arthur Schopenhauer, known as the father of pessimism, took such a negative view of life you would expect suicide to be the logical conclusion to his philosophy. He opposed suicide, however, considering it a foolish and useless act, although he insisted that people have a right to take their lives if they want to. A better way to cope with the hardships of life, he taught, is to live an ascetic existence that makes no demands on life and has no expectations of it.

Friedrich Nietzsche, who was influenced by Schopenhauer, also supported a person's moral right to commit suicide. Nietzsche, who constantly suffered from physical and mental illness and had a severe mental breakdown toward the end of his life, often contemplated suicide himself. "The thought of suicide," he wrote, "is a strong consolation: it helps to get over many a bad night." But Nietzsche did not advocate suicide as a solution to all of life's problems. He also affirmed life, and maintained that "suffering is no argument against life."

Nietzsche, Schopenhauer, and other philosophers of the late 1800s moved far away from religious teachings in their philosophies and in their attitudes toward suicide. Other thinkers and writers struggled with the implications of giving up traditional religious beliefs in God and in a world after death. What meaning does any life have, they wondered, if in the end we simply die and fade into nothingness? And if life has no meaning does suicide become not only a right, but a necessity?

The American philosopher and psychologist William James attacked the question head on in an address called "Is Life Worth Living?" that he delivered in 1895 to the Harvard Young Men's Christian Association. James understood well the suicidal impulses that can overtake a person, because he himself had suffered severe clinical depression as a young man. He spoke of those feelings in his lecture and of the "nightmare view of life" that can overwhelm people as they ponder their own existence and question the very purpose of life.

His answer to the question "Is life worth living?" was a roundly affirmative "Yes." Although nobody can prove God exists or that reason guides the course of the universe, anybody can make a positive decision to believe those things, said James. "Believe that life is worth living," advised the philosopher, "and your belief will help to create the fact."

Forty-five years after James's lecture, the French novelist and essayist Albert Camus analyzed many of the same problems in his essay "The Myth of Sisyphus." "There is but one truly serious philosophical problem," said Camus, "and that is suicide." Life, to Camus, is absurd, and the proof of the absurdity of life is death, which annihilates life. Because life ultimately ends in death and does not go beyond death, all its struggles, all its aspirations, all its vanities are meaningless. Does it not logically follow, asked Camus, that if life has no meaning it is not worth living, and that suicide must be the only course of action that makes sense?

To this question the answer was "No." The meaninglessness of life does not necessarily lead to the conclusion that it is not worth living. On the contrary, Camus argued, the meaninglessness of life provides all the more reason for living. By celebrating life, by living it to the fullest, and by dying "not of one's free will," people can triumph over the meaninglessness of life and the absurdity of fate.

The works of Freud, Durkheim, and other psychiatrists and sociologists of the 1900s shifted interest from religious and moral arguments about suicide to investigations into its causes and prevention. In our own times, however, many of the old questions about the rightness

147

or wrongness of suicide have been raised again. And now they extend far beyond theoretical discussions to everyday medical, legal, and personal decisions.

At the heart of the debate today is the question of whether people should be allowed the "right to die" if they so wish it, without interference from others. In its narrow sense the question relates essentially to people who are terminally ill or in great pain and agony, and for whom no hope of improvement exists. In its broadest sense it extends to any person who chooses to end life.

People who oppose any kind of death by choice argue that life should be preserved as long as possible, no matter what the circumstances. Even when people are terminally ill, they maintain, nobody can really determine at what moment life loses all meaning and hope. They point to seemingly miraculous recoveries made by sick persons who might have been left to die if laws did not force physicians to keep life going as long as possible. These people insist, too, that condoning any kind of suicide, for any reason, condones all suicides, and that society does not have the moral right to approve of suicide.

Those people who would allow a terminally ill person to choose death in order to avoid further suffering argue that dramatic medical advances have altered the natural processes of life. Physicians can now prolong life to the point at which it no longer has meaning, and existence becomes simply a matter of the proper functioning of a series of medical gadgets. At that point, these people say, a person's body is too debilitated for a "miracle" cure or a sudden medical discovery to reverse the course of illness. At that point, the person should be allowed to give up the gadgets if he or she so wishes. And physicians should be permitted to accede to the person's wishes in order to allow death to come peacefully and with dignity.

Most people who support the concept of death by

choice make a clear distinction between allowing old or sick persons to choose death when they wish and allowing suicide among the general population. "Death by choice in a medical context," writes Daniel C. Maguire, a Roman Catholic theologian, in his book *Death by Choice,* "is a different reality to the point where it must be treated and judged separately. My position is that, with suicide as with war, there are massive presumptions against its moral rightness."

But a small number of physicians, scholars, and lay people insist that all persons have the right to control their own bodies, to live or die as they wish. Choosing to die, they say, is not morally wrong, but it is morally wrong to prevent people who want to die from doing so.

Most extreme and vocal among the advocates of the "right to suicide" is Thomas Szasz, a maverick psychiatrist who has argued that physicians hold too much power over mentally ill patients. Dr. Szasz believes that any person who wants to commit suicide should be allowed to do so without intervention from others unless that person asks for help. He strongly opposes involuntary hospitalization or forced treatment for suicidal persons even when it is clear the person will take his or her life without treatment. "In a free society," says Szasz in his book *Law, Liberty, and Psychiatry,* "a person must have the right to injure or kill himself . . . there is no moral justification for depriving a person of his liberty in order to treat him."

Ultimately each person must choose his or her own answers to the philosophic questions of whether suicide is morally right or whether it ever can be justified. But the question of whether a suicidal person should receive treatment is not strictly a philosophic one. It's a medical and social one that involves recognized facts. And these facts need to be kept in mind so that the concept of a "right to suicide" doesn't get carried to a misleading and dangerous extreme.

The basic facts are that no one is suicidal all the time and no one—except perhaps the very old and very ill—is totally committed to bringing about his or her own death. The suicidal mood swings back and forth. People vary from moment to moment in their suicidal intent. A teenage boy who speaks of suicide may be speaking out of blinding depression and a confusion of thoughts and motives. If, by ignoring hints and clues and not intervening, you allow such a person the freedom to carry out his act, you essentially take away his freedom to change his mind. Under the guise of a philosophic right you betray a medical truth: that is, that every person who wants to die also wants to live. The part of a suicidal person that cries out for life needs to be responded to even while the other part must be respected.

In answering the author's survey question, "Do you think suicide among young people is ever justified?" a college freshman answered "No," and then explained that she had been taking drugs, had attempted suicide, and then had entered therapy. She went on:

"Now that I am well on my way to getting my head on straight finally, after all these years, I can honestly say that I feel that no matter what kind of bind you are in you should try your damnedest to get out of it, get yourself together, mentally and physically. Most people who have been using drugs or drinking and have become suicidal need therapy and someone to talk to. I myself see a social worker.

"No one can make you want to live. But believe me, life is too precious to throw away. I know. I would never be so foolish again. I'm just glad I faced up to myself. Now I *love* me."

10 Preventing Young Suicides

Can We Stop the Epidemic?

"My boyfriend left me. He says he never wants to see me again. We went together for two years. I'm carrying his baby, and now he left me."

"Is there anyone in your family who can help you?"

"My mother would kill me if she knew."

"What will you do?"

"I'll kill myself first."

The conversation took place at a suicide prevention center in a midwestern city. The girl called the center because she had no place else to turn for help. A trained volunteer answered her phone call, and arranged to get her the help she needed.

Spread throughout the United States some two hundred suicide prevention centers help people like this teenage girl cope with life crises that threaten to overwhelm them. The trained volunteers and therapists who work at these centers provide a lifeline for people who call them, pulling them in out of their immediate suicidal crises and offering them relief and some hope for the future.

The centers serve as one major line of defense

against the suicide epidemic. A person in need can call a local center at any time of day or night and receive help. Each year thousands of persons, young and old, make such calls. In New York City, about 8,000 persons a year call National Save-A-Life League. More than 12,000 persons call the Los Angeles Suicide Prevention Center each year and about 20,000 call San Francisco Suicide Prevention. And even in idyllic Honolulu, Hawaii, more than 20,000 persons call the Suicide and Crisis Center. The centers try to publicize their numbers. Generally, too, you can find a local center number by looking under "Suicide" in the phone book. (Appendix B lists the names and numbers of suicide prevention centers throughout the United States.)

The centers regard themselves as first-aid stations for suicide prevention, and have limited their services accordingly. They help callers cope with emergencies and immediate crises. They do not try to provide long-term therapy to change a lifetime of habits or remake a caller's personality. But for such therapy they may refer callers to professional psychiatrists, psychologists, social workers, or counselors whose names are listed with the center.

If you spent even one day at a center you could probably get a good idea of the kinds of problems its staff members handle every day and every night. You might hear a telephone volunteer speaking to a frightened unwed teenager who has become pregnant, like the one described above. Or you might listen in as a center counselor sets up an appointment for a distraught man to visit a psychiatric clinic at a nominal fee. Or, in an extreme emergency, you might become caught up in the drama of speeding a police officer to the home of a teenage boy who is threatening to blow off his head while he talks to the telephone therapist.

Some centers estimate that about a third of their

calls come from suicidal people, some of them dangerously near suicide. About a third come from people going through other kinds of crises from which they want aid or a referral to someone who can help them. And about a third of the calls a center gets come from people who are lonely and sad and "just want to talk."

Most centers have a few professional people—psychiatrists, psychologists, or social workers—who spend part time or full time at the center. Most staff members, however, are either trained volunteers or paid counselors who have been trained for the job. All the people connected with a center take part in an intensive training program to learn how to handle the emergency problems they constantly face. They are taught to take a case history over the phone and to ask leading questions to determine how serious a suicide threat is. How old is the caller? Has she or he made detailed suicide plans? Has a method been chosen, a time set? The center therapists learn quickly that the more specific a suicidal plan and the greater the number of details that have been thought out, the more dangerous the situation.

The idea of a community center to help prevent suicide goes back to the year 1906, when two such centers opened in different parts of the world. One, National-Save-A-Life League in New York City, began with a small staff trained by its founder, Baptist minister Harry M. Warren. The founder's son, Harry Warren, directs that center today, following many of the guidelines established by his father. The second center, set up in England by the Salvation Army, aimed at treating people after they had attempted suicide rather than trying to intervene before they made attempts. The Army's anti-suicide department still exists, but much of its work has been taken over by other organizations in England.

The Samaritans, one of the major suicide prevention

organizations in England, has opened centers in several parts of the world. The Reverend Chad Varah started the organization in London in 1953 around the idea of befriending people in trouble. Many of the volunteers who run Samaritan centers are former suicide attempters who work with suicidal people in much the same way that former alcoholics work with new members of Alcoholics Anonymous. The volunteers try to serve as substitute families or close friends to the people who come to them, offering love, care, and companionship. They almost never refer people to mental hospitals, and only rarely do they refer them to professional therapists or psychiatrists.

When psychologists Edwin Shneidman and Norman Farberow began the Los Angeles Suicide Prevention Center in 1958, they opened with an all-professional staff. As time went on, they admitted volunteers to the program. Today the center has about 150 telephone volunteers who answer about 1,000 calls a month.

Led by Shneidman and Farberow, the Los Angeles center became the wellspring for much of the research that has been done about suicide and suicide prevention. One of the most important research tools that grew out of the center was the "psychological autopsy," a method to help coroners determine the cause of death when it is not clearly indicated.

In equivocal cases, members of the center's "death investigation team" interview friends and relatives, teachers, co-workers and anyone else who may have played a significant role in the person's life. They review the victim's actions in the days and hours before death, and try to get an overall picture of the person's character, personality, and state of mind. On the basis of the data they gather, team members judge whether the person died accidentally or intentionally or whether the death might have been a subintentioned one, in which the person unconsciously wanted to die. They

154

report their findings to the coroner, who incorporates them into his own post-mortem investigation and decides whether to list the death as homicide, suicide, or accident.

The Los Angeles center also became the model for the many other centers that began to appear throughout the United States. Today the American Association of Suicidology coordinates the work of all the suicide prevention centers. The association publishes a journal called *Suicide and Life-Threatening Behavior,* and develops standards for accrediting the work of prevention centers. It also helps local centers plan publicity and educational programs.

At some centers counselors and volunteers go into the community to spread suicide prevention information. Some suicide prevention people work closely with prison officials, who must cope with especially high rates of suicide and suicide attempts among young male prisoners. Increasing numbers of suicide prevention centers have joined forces with other crisis intervention centers and "hot lines" that handle such problems as rape, drug abuse, and accidental poisonings.

Many countries of the world have suicide prevention centers similar to those of the United States and England. Suicide rates in many of these countries are much higher than in the United States, which ranks sixteenth highest in the world with a rate of 12.0 per 100,000. Hungary and Austria, for example, report rates almost twice as high.

In spite of the centers' many activities, some sociologists and psychologists have leveled strong criticism against them. Their main complaint is that the centers do not reach the most seriously suicidal people in society. People who call in, they say, are not those most desperately in need of help. Desperate people don't make phone calls; they act on their impulses. Critics of the centers back their arguments with statistics that

155

show that U.S. centers have not brought about reduced suicide rates in areas in which they operate.

Suicide prevention people respond to the charges by pointing out that they answer the calls of thousands of people. Even if these people do not represent the "hard-core" suicides, they are people who need and want help. Many of them feel too threatened by "officialdom" of the medical and psychiatric world to seek professional help on their own. They don't need to make an appointment to call a center, and they don't need to fill out forbidding forms before someone will speak to them. They simply lift the phone and dial, and nobody even makes them give their names if they don't want to. If these people did not have centers to call many would become more unhappy, isolated, and frightened, and perhaps join the ranks of the more seriously suicidal. Each call answered, each person reached, may represent a life saved in the future.

Beyond the work at the centers, research into the causes of and cures for suicide goes on at many levels. Nationally, the National Institute of Mental Health offers grants and funds to qualified researchers to study suicide problems. Internationally, the World Health Organization collects statistics, holds international meetings on suicide research, and publishes and distributes books that grow from those meetings. The International Association of Suicide Prevention also holds worldwide meetings at which suicide prevention leaders from many countries exchange information.

Research goes on. Prevention centers grow busier and busier. Each researcher, each volunteer counselor, each therapist who treats a suicidal patient chops away bit by bit at the mystery of suicide. But the numbers of young people who die by their own hands continue to rise.

Suicide ranks as the second or third killer of the young in almost every industrialized country of the world. One of the reasons it has risen to such a high position of fatality in the United States and elsewhere is that medical science has conquered many other diseases that once destroyed young lives. You rarely, if ever, hear of a young person dying today of polio, scarlet fever, tuberculosis, or diphtheria, as thousands of young people did years ago. As these illnesses have moved out of the ranks of destructiveness, suicide has moved up in importance. Among older people, diseases such as cancer and heart ailments still claim many more lives than suicide.

But the very fact that many serious childhood diseases have been almost wiped out while suicide rates for young people have increased steadily does call attention to the great difficulties that have impeded efforts to prevent suicide. Mass private and public support helped conquer the old fatal diseases. Rich and prominent people held charity balls to raise money for their favorite cause, and the not-so-rich contributed as they could to the dozens of fund-raising campaigns conducted. Over the years the federal government allotted vast amounts of money to study the diseases and distribute information about them.

No such widespread private and public support has been mobilized to fight suicide. No charity balls or door-to-door fund-raising campaigns have taken place. And although the federal government has granted funds for individuals and institutions to study suicide, it has not set aside the large sums of money for suicide research that it has for research in other life-threatening areas.

Consider these figures. In 1976 Congress appropriated almost $744 million for research into cancer, a disease for which about a million and a half Americans are treated each year. Only slightly more than $5 million was appropriated for research into clinical depression, although it affects between four and eight million Americans a year and is one of the most important precursors of suicide.

For most people suicide remains today what it has always been: a "closet" affliction. People speak of it in whispers, and hide it from others. They feel ashamed when it occurs and most ashamed when a young person becomes the victim. Yet if we want to stop the suicide epidemic we must break the conspiracy of silence that surrounds it. Youthful suicides need to be recognized as a major public health problem and treated as such by government, professionals, and the general public. As a subject, suicide among the young needs to be researched in and of itself, apart from the characteristics of suicide in general. And information about it needs to be made available to everyone, young people and older ones.

Not too long ago people regarded cancer as a kind of "social disease" to be kept secret from everybody, including the person who suffered from it. Many people shied away from using the word cancer. They spoke of it as "C.A." or "you know what." Then the American Cancer Society and other organizations began large-scale campaigns to publicize information about the disease. People learned to recognize symptoms and to act on their discoveries early enough to allow for cures. Publicity about breast cancer alone, for example, has saved the lives of hundreds of women who have mastered techniques of self-examination and are not afraid to seek treatment before the illness spreads.

In the same way, early symptoms that may lead to young suicides can be publicized and taught. Friends, teachers, parents, and others can learn to recognize some of the symptoms of depression or the warning signals for deep psychological disturbance. They can

158

learn the simple facts: that people who talk about suicide *do* attempt it; that most people who complete suicide *have* made one or more previous attempts. And they can learn to recognize when someone needs professional treatment, and how to help them get that treatment.

Young people themselves need to learn to recognize the clues to suicide among their friends and relatives. And they need to be made aware of the importance of telling others if they suspect someone they know has become suicidal. High school and college students have responded with great interest to courses about death and dying offered in some schools. Such courses should be offered to all students.

Parents need suicide information that emphasizes the importance of the early years in a child's development, and the many subtle ways children can be made to feel unloved and unwanted. Parents should also be made aware of the effects divorce, death, or suicide in the family may have on a child, and learn how to ease the hardships these events may cause. If you look on the bookshelves of any bookstore, you will find dozens of books about child-rearing. But if you turn to the indexes of these books, you will rarely find an entry under "suicide." The subject of suicide needs to be covered in popular literature, in the everyday magazines and guidance books parents read.

Teachers need to know about the depressions of childhood and the ways young people often mask their sadness and loneliness with angry, disruptive behavior. This information should be made available even to nursery-school and kindergarten teachers, who can often help a child before symptoms become solidified. Upper-grade teachers need to learn not to be afraid to discuss problems of suicide with their students; not to "hush up" a suicide or attempted suicide in a school

159

but to face it openly, and allow students to air their feelings.

Other professionals too—doctors, priests, ministers, rabbis—need to have more information about young suicides made available to them. People turn to them for help, yet they themselves often feel threatened and uncomfortable when faced with a suicide problem.

It would be naive and foolish to pretend that suicide among the young can be abolished simply by educating people and spreading more information about it, or even by conducting more and better research into the subject. So many social and psychological forces affect young suicides that no single action can possibly solve the problem. A spiraling divorce rate, chaotic homes, confusion about religious beliefs and moral values, shrinking family groups, feelings of alienation between men and women and between young and old—all these bring pressure and confusion and despair to young people. The causes that create young suicides need to be dealt with along with any other attempts to stop the rising rates.

But changes in society develop over time. And every day ten more young people take their own lives; a thousand more attempt to. If just one extra life can be saved because a friend has learned how to help, if just two suicide attempts can be avoided because parents have picked up clues, a beginning will have been made.

Appendix A

Rise in Suicide Rates Among the Young,

Ages 15–24, United States, 1956–1977

Source: Division of Vital Statistics, U.S. Public Health Service

Year   Suicide Rates per 100,000 population in each group

	TOTAL			WHITE			OTHER RACES		
	Both Sexes	Male	Female	Both Sexes	Male	Female	Both Sexes	Male	Female
1977	13.6	21.8	5.3	14.3	22.9	5.5	9.6	15.5	4.0
1976	11.7	18.5	4.8	12.1	19.2	4.9	9.3	14.7	4.0
1975	11.8	18.9	4.8	12.3	19.6	4.9	9.1	14.4	3.9
1974	10.9	17.1	4.6	11.4	17.8	4.8	8.3	12.9	3.9
1973	10.6	17.0	4.3	10.9	17.4	4.3	8.9	14.0	4.1
1972	10.2	15.7	4.7	10.1	15.5	4.6	10.0	16.7	5.6
1971	9.4	14.1	4.7	9.6	14.5	4.6	8.4	11.5	5.3
1970	8.8	13.5	4.2	9.0	13.9	4.3	7.6	11.3	4.1
1969	8.0	12.3	3.8	8.1	12.6	3.8	6.9	9.9	4.1
1968	7.1	10.9	3.4	7.3	11.3	3.4	5.6	8.2	3.1
1967	7.0	10.5	3.5	7.1	10.8	3.4	6.1	8.2	4.0
1966	6.4	9.7	3.1	6.5	9.9	3.2	5.7	8.6	2.9
1965	6.2	9.4	3.0	6.3	9.6	3.0	5.8	8.5	3.1
1964	6.0	9.2	2.8	6.1	9.3	2.9	4.9	8.0	2.0
1963	6.0	9.0	3.1	6.2	9.2	3.1	5.0	7.5	2.6
1962	5.7	8.5	2.9	5.8	8.7	2.9	5.2	7.5	3.0
1961	5.1	7.9	2.3	5.1	7.9	2.3	4.7	7.6	2.0
1960	5.2	8.2	2.2	5.4	8.6	2.3	3.4	5.3	1.5
1959	4.9	7.7	2.1	5.0	7.9	2.1	4.3	6.6	2.2
1958	4.8	7.4	2.3	5.0	7.6	2.4	3.5	5.4	1.7
1957	4.0	6.4	1.8	4.1	6.5	1.8	3.4	5.6	1.4
1956	4.0	6.3	1.9	4.1	6.4	2.0	3.4	5.8	1.2

Appendix B

Suicide Prevention/Crisis Intervention

Agencies in the United States

ALABAMA

Crisis Center of Jefferson
  County, Inc.
3600 Eighth Avenue South
BIRMINGHAM, ALABAMA
  35222
Phone: (205) 323-7777

Riverbend Center for
  Mental Health
635 West College Street
FLORENCE, ALABAMA
  35631
Phone: (205) 764-3431

ALASKA

Suicide Prevention & Crisis
  Center
825 L Street
ANCHORAGE, ALASKA
  99501
Phone: (907) 277-0222

ARIZONA

Suicide Prevention Service
  for Maricopa County
2601 East Roosevelt
PHOENIX, ARIZONA
  85006
Phone: (602) 275-3667

Help On Call
2302 East Speedway
TUCSON, ARIZONA 85719
Phone: (602) 323-9373

CALIFORNIA

Melody Land Hot Line
ANAHEIM, CALIFORNIA
  92805
Phone: (714) 778-1000

Suicide Prevention of
  Alameda County, Inc.

P.O. Box 9102
BERKELEY, CALIFORNIA
94709
Phone: North County (415)
849-2212
South County (415)
537-1324

Hot-Line Garden Grove
12345 Euclid Street
GARDEN GROVE, CALI-
FORNIA 92640
Phone: (714) 827-2466

Suicide Prevention of Santa
Cruz County, Inc.
P.O. Box 734
CAPITOLA, CALIFORNIA
95010
Phone: (408) 426-2342
(408) 688-6581

West Orange County Hot
Line
P.O. Box 32
LOS ALAMITOS, CALI-
FORNIA 90720
Phone: (213) 596-5548
(714) 761-4575
(714) 894-4242

Monterey County Suicide
Prevention Center
P.O. Box 3241
CARMEL, CALIFORNIA
93921
Phone: (408) 649-8008
(408) 424-1485

Help Line Contact Clinic
427 West Fifth Street,
Suite 500
LOS ANGELES, CALI-
FORNIA 90013
Phone: (213) 620-0144

Suicide Prevention
618 Sunset Court
DAVIS, CALIFORNIA
95616
Phone: (916) 756-5000/5001

Crisis Intervention Center
127 West Main Street
EL CAJON, CALIFORNIA
92020
Phone: (714) 444-1194/1195

Suicide Prevention Center
1041 South Menlo Avenue
LOS ANGELES, CALIFOR-
NIA 90006
Phone: (213) 381-5111

North Bay Suicide
  Prevention, Inc.
P.O. Box 2444
NAPA, CALIFORNIA
  94558
Phone: (707) 643-2555
          (Vallejo)
        (707) 255-2555
          (Napa)
        (707) 963-2555
          (St. Helena)

Desert Hospital Outpatient
1150 North India
PALM SPRINGS,
  CALIFORNIA 92262
Phone: (714) 346-9502

Pasadena Mental Health
  Association
1495 North Lake Avenue
PASADENA, CALIFORNIA
  91104
Phone: (213) 798-0907/
        0908/0909

Psychiatric Emergency
  Services
2315 Stockton Boulevard
SACRAMENTO,
  CALIFORNIA 95817
Phone: (916) 453-3696

Suicide Prevention Service
P.O. Box 449, 331 J Street
SACRAMENTO,
  CALIFORNIA 95802
Phone: (209) 223-1859

Marin Suicide Prevention
  Center, Inc.
P.O. Box 792
SAN ANSELMO,
  CALIFORNIA 94960
Phone: (415) 454-4524/4525

Defy Counseling Line
2870 4th Avenue
SAN DIEGO, CALIFORNIA
Phone: (714) 236-3339

Help Center
5069 College Avenue
SAN DIEGO, CALIFORNIA
  92115
Phone: (714) 582-HELP;
        582-4442

San Francisco Suicide
  Prevention, Inc.
307 12th Avenue
SAN FRANCISCO,
  CALIFORNIA 94118
Phone: (415) 221-1421

Center for Special Problems
2107 Van Ness Avenue
SAN FRANCISCO,
  CALIFORNIA 94109
Phone: (415) 558-4801

Suicide and Crisis Service
645 South Bascom Avenue
SAN JOSE, CALIFORNIA
  95128
Phone: (408) 287-2424

164

Suicide Prevention Center
274 West 20th Street
SAN MATEO,
   CALIFORNIA 94403
Phone: (415) 349-HOPE

Ventura County Suicide
   Prevention Service
4900 Telegraph Road
VENTURA, CALIFORNIA
   93003
Phone: (805) 648-2444

Contra Costa Suicide
   Prevention
P.O. Box 4852
WALNUT CREEK,
   CALIFORNIA 94596
Phone: (415) 939-3232

COLORADO

Aurora Community Mental
   Health Center
1646 Elmira
AURORA, COLORADO
   80010
Phone: (303) 344-9260

Suicide Referral Service
12 North Meade
COLORADO SPRINGS,
   COLORADO 80930
Phone: (303) 471-4357

Emergency Psychiatric
   Service, Colorado General
   Hospital
4200 East Ninth Avenue
DENVER, COLORADO
   80220
Phone: (303) 394-8297

Emergency Room Psychiatric
   Services, Denver General
   Hospital
West Eighth Avenue and
   Bannock
DENVER, COLORADO
   80206
Phone: (303) 244-6835

Suicide and Crisis Control
2459 South Ash
DENVER, COLORADO
   80222
Phone: (303) 756-8485
            757-0988; 789-3073

Arapahoe Mental Health
   Center
4857 South Broadway
ENGLEWOOD,
   COLORADO 80110
Phone: (303) 761-0620

Suicide Prevention Service
   and Crisis Center
812 Rood Avenue
GRAND JUNCTION,
   COLORADO 81501
Phone: (303) 242-2255

Pueblo Suicide Prevention
   Center
1600 West 24th Street
PUEBLO, COLORADO
   81003
Phone: (303) 544-1133

CONNECTICUT

Mental Health Center
BRIDGEPORT,
   CONNECTICUT 06610
Phone: (203) 333-3589

DELAWARE

Psychiatric Emergency Help
   Line Clinic
Georgetown State Service
   Center
GEORGETOWN,
   DELAWARE 19947
Phone: (302) 856-6626

DISTRICT OF COLUMBIA

Suicide Prevention and
   Emergency Mental Health
1905 E Street, S.E.
WASHINGTON, D.C.
   20002
Phone: (202) 727-3622

Washington D.C. Hotline
Phone: (202) 462-6690

FLORIDA

Suicide and Crisis
   Intervention Service, Inc.
606 Third Avenue
GAINESVILLE, FLORIDA
   32601
Phone: (904) 376-4444

We Care, Inc.
112 Passadena Park
ORLANDO, FLORIDA
   32801
Phone: (305) 628-1227

Crisis and Suicide
   Intervention Service
1770 Cedar Street
ROCKLEDGE, FLORIDA
   32955
Phone: (305) 784-2433

Crisis Line
4204 Manatee Avenue
SARASOTA, FLORIDA
   33578
Phone: (813) 748-8585

Crisis Line
1301 Lake Avenue
LAKE WATER, FLORIDA
   33460
Phone: North line,
      (305) 588-1121;
      South line,
      (305) 272-1121

GEORGIA

Emergency Mental Health
  Service
265 Boulevard
ATLANTA, GEORGIA
  30312
Phone: (404) 572-2626

Carroll Crisis Intervention
  Center
827 Maple Street
CARROLLTON, GEORGIA
  30117
Phone: (404) 834-3326/3327

Helpline
1512 Bull Street
SAVANNAH, GEORGIA
  31401
Phone: (912) 232-3383

HAWAII

Suicide and Crisis Center
200 North Vineyard
  Boulevard, Room 603
HONOLULU, HAWAII
  96817
Phone: (808) 521-4555

ILLINOIS

Call For Help
7623 West Main
BELLEVILLE, ILLINOIS
  62223
Phone: (618) 397-0963

Suicide Prevention and Crisis
  Service
1206 South Randolph
CHAMPAIGN, ILLINOIS
  61820
Phone: (217) 359-4141

Crisis Intervention Program
Chicago-Reed Mental Health
  Service
4200 North Oak Park
  Avenue
CHICAGO, ILLINOIS
  60634
Phone: (312) 794-3609

Crisis Counseling Service
601 N. 18 Street
MOUNT VERNON,
  ILLINOIS 62864
Phone: (618) 242-1512

Call For Help
PEORIA, ILLINOIS
Phone: (309) 691-7373/7374

Suicide Prevention Service
4409 Main Street
QUINCY, ILLINOIS 62301
Phone: (217) 222-1166

Open Line Service
908 East Cherry Street
WATSEKA, ILLINOIS
  60970
Phone: (815) 432-5111

INDIANA

Crisis and Suicide Interven-
   tion Service
1433 North Meridian Street
INDIANAPOLIS,
   INDIANA 46202
Phone: (317) 632-7575

IOWA

Lee County Mental Health
   Center
1013 Concert Street
KEOKUK, IOWA 52632
Phone: (319) 524-3873

KANSAS

Area Mental Health Center
156 Gardendale
GARDEN CITY, KANSAS
   67846
Phone: (316) 276-7689

North Mental Clinic
1801 East 10th Street
WICHITA, KANSAS 67214
Phone: (316) 268-8251

LOUISIANA

The Phone
Student Health Service,
   Louisiana State University
BATON ROUGE,
   LOUISIANA 70803
Phone: (504) 388-8222/1234

Crisis Line
1528 Jackson Avenue
NEW ORLEANS,
   LOUISIANA 70130
Phone: (504) 523-2673

MAINE

DIAL HELP
The Counseling Center
43 Illinois Avenue
BANGOR, MAINE 04401
Phone: Watts Toll Free
   Number 1-800-432-
   7810

Ingraham Volunteers, Inc.
142 High Street
PORTLAND, MAINE
   04101
Phone: (207) 773-5516

MARYLAND

Crisis Intervention of Sinai
   Hospital
Belvedere Avenue at
   Greenspring
BALTIMORE,
   MARYLAND 21215
Phone: (301) 367-7800

MASSACHUSETTS

Project Place—Hot Line
32 Rutland Street
BOSTON,
   MASSACHUSETTS 02118
Phone: (617) 267-9150

168

Samaritans of Boston
802 Boylston
BOSTON,
    MASSACHUSETTS 02199
Phone: (617) 247-0220

MICHIGAN

Suicide Prevention Center
1151 Taylor Avenue
DETROIT, MICHIGAN
    48202
Phone: (313) 875-5466

Suicide Prevention Crisis
    Intervention Service
Ottawa County Community
    Mental Health
GRAND HAVEN,
    MICHIGAN 49417
Phone: (616) 842-4357

Ottawa County Community
    Mental Health
12265 James Street
HOLLAND, MICHIGAN
    49423
Phone: (616) 396-4537;
    458-4357

Crisis Intervention
1619 Fort Street
LINCOLN PARK,
    MICHIGAN 48146
Phone: (313) 383-9000

MINNESOTA

Crisis Intervention Center
Hennepin Medical Center
701 Park Avenue South
MINNEAPOLIS,
    MINNESOTA 55415
Phone: (612) 347-2222

Youth Emergency Services
MINNEAPOLIS,
    MINNESOTA
Phone: (612) 339-7033

MISSISSIPPI

Weems Mental Health
    Center
P.O. Box 4376 West Station
MERIDIAN, MISSISSIPPI
    39301
Phone: (601) 483-4821

MISSOURI

St. Francis Community
    Mental Health Center
211 St. Francis Drive
CAPE GIRARDEAU,
    MISSOURI 63701
Phone: (314) 334-6400

Crisis Intervention, Inc.
P.O. Box 582
JOPLIN, MISSOURI 64801
Phone: (417) 781-2255

Western Missouri Suicide
   Prevention Center
600 East 22nd Street
KANSAS CITY, MISSOURI
   64108
Phone: (816) 471-3000

St. Joseph Suicide
   Prevention Service
St. Joseph State Hospital
ST. JOSEPH, MISSOURI
   64502
Phone: (816) 232-1655

Suicide Prevention, Inc.
1118 Hampton Avenue
ST. LOUIS, MISSOURI
   63139
Phone: (314) 725-2010

MONTANA

Blackfeet Crisis Center
Blackfeet Reservation
BROWNING, MONTANA
   59417
Phone: (406) 338-5525

Great Falls Crisis Center
P.O. Box 124
GREAT FALLS,
   MONTANA 59401
Phone: (406) 453-6511

NEVADA

Suicide Prevention and Crisis
   Call Center
Room 206, Mack SS Building
University of Nevada
RENO, NEVADA
Phone: (702) 323-6111

NEW HAMPSHIRE

Androscoggin Valley Mental
   Health Center
P.O. Box 276,
   Page Hill Road
BERLIN, NEW
   HAMPSHIRE 03570
Phone: (603) 752-7404

Central New Hampshire
   Community Health
   Services, Inc.
5 Market Lane
CONCORD, NEW
   HAMPSHIRE 03301
Phone: (603) 228-1551

NEW JERSEY

Crisis Intervention Center
ATLANTIC CITY,
   NEW JERSEY 08401
Phone: (609) 344-1118

Emergency Service Guidance
   Center of Camden County
19 East Ormond Avenue
CHERRY HILL,
   NEW JERSEY 08034
Phone: (609) 428-4357

Screening-Crisis Intervention
1129B Woodlane Road
MT. HOLLY,
   NEW JERSEY 08060
Phone: (609) 764-1100

NEW MEXICO

Suicide Emergency Services
2600 Marble N.E.
ALBUQUERQUE, NEW
   MEXICO 87106
Phone: (505) 265-7557

The Bridge Crisis
   Intervention Center
113 Bridge Street
LAS VEGAS, NEW
   MEXICO 87701
Phone: (505) 425-6793

NEW YORK

Suicide Prevention Service
Kings County Hospital
   Center
600 Winthrop Street
BROOKLYN, NEW YORK
   11203
Phone: (212) 462-3322

Mental Health Association
   of Nassau County
186 Clinton Street
HEMPSTEAD, NEW YORK
   11550
Phone: (516) 489-2322

Suicide Prevention of
   Tompkins County, Inc.
P.O. Box 312
ITHACA, NEW YORK
   14850
Phone: (607) 272-1616

Help Line
3 West 29th Street
NEW YORK, NEW YORK
   10001
Phone: (212) 532-2400

National Save-A-Life
   League, Inc.
815 Second Avenue
NEW YORK, NEW YORK
   10017
Phone: (212) 736-6191

Niagara Drug Abuse and
   Crisis Intervention
Old County Building
Third and Cedar
NIAGARA FALLS, NEW
   YORK 14303
Phone: (716) 285-3515

Lifeline
601 Elmwood Avenue,
   Box 321
ROCHESTER, NEW YORK
   14642
Phone: (716) 275-5151

Suicide Prevention Center
29 Sterling Avenue
WHITE PLAINS, NEW
   YORK 10606
Phone: (914) 946-0121

NORTH CAROLINA

Crisis Control Center, Inc.
P.O. Box 735
GREENSBORO, NORTH
   CAROLINA 27402
Phone: (919) 275-2852

Crisis Line
JACKSONVILLE, NORTH
   CAROLINA 28540
Phone: (919) 353-6666

Crisis and Suicide
Intervention
P.O. Box Q
SANFORD, NORTH
CAROLINA 27330
Phone: (919) 776-5431

NORTH DAKOTA

Suicide Prevention and
Emergency Service
Ninth and Thayer
BISMARCK, NORTH
DAKOTA 58501
Phone: (701) 255-4124

Suicide Prevention and
Mental Health Center
108 Eighth Street South
FARGO, NORTH
DAKOTA 58103
Phone: (701) 232-4357

OHIO

Support, Inc.
1361 West Market Street
AKRON, OHIO 44313
Phone: (216) 434-9144

Intervention Center of
Stark County, Inc.
1341 North Market
CANTON, OHIO 44714
Phone: (216) 452-9811

Suicide Prevention
COLUMBUS, OHIO 43215
Phone: (614) 221-5445/5451

Suicide Prevention Service
184 Salem Avenue
DAYTON, OHIO 45406
Phone: (513) 223-4777

Town Hall II, Help Line
225 East College Street
KENT, OHIO 44240
Phone: (216) 672-4357

Crisis Hotline
2845 Bell Street
ZANESVILLE, OHIO 43701
Phone: (614) 452-8403

OREGON

Crisis Service
127 N.A. Sixth Street
CORVALLIS, OREGON
97330
Phone: (503) 752-7030

Crisis Center
University of Oregon
Counseling Center
EUGENE, OREGON 97403
Phone: (503) 686-4488

PENNSYLVANIA

Lifeline
520 East Broad Street
BETHLEHEM,
PENNSYLVANIA 18018
Phone: (215) 691-0660

Suicide and Crisis
   Intervention Service
PHILADELPHIA,
   PENNSYLVANIA
Phone: (215) 686-4420

SOUTH CAROLINA

Crisis Intervention Service
GREENVILLE, SOUTH
   CAROLINA 29605
Phone: (803) 271-0220

TENNESSEE

Crisis Intervention Service
1520 Cherokee Trail
KNOXVILLE, TENNESSEE
   37920
Phone: (615) 637-9711

Suicide Prevention Service
P.O. Box 4068
MEMPHIS, TENNESSEE
   38104
Phone: (901) 274-7473

Crisis Intervention Center,
   Inc.
250 Venture Circle
NASHVILLE, TENNESSEE
   37208
Phone: (615) 244-7444

TEXAS

Suicide Prevention
Box 3044
AMARILLO, TEXAS 79106
Phone: (806) 376-4251

Suicide Prevention-Crisis
   Service
P.O. Box 375
CORPUS CHRISTI, TEXAS
   78404
Phone: (512) 883-6244/6245

Suicide Prevention of Dallas,
   Inc.
P.O. Box 19651
DALLAS, TEXAS 75219
Phone: (214) 521-5531

Crisis Services
P.O. Box 9997
EL PASO, TEXAS 79990
Phone: (915) 779-1800

Crisis Intervention Service of
   Tarrant County
600 Texas Street
FORT WORTH, TEXAS
   76102
Phone: (817) 336-3355

Concern
P.O. Box 1945
WICHITA FALLS, TEXAS
   76301
Phone: (817) 723-0821

UTAH

Granite Community Mental
   Health Center
156 Westminster Avenue
SALT LAKE CITY, UTAH
   84115
Phone: (801) 487-5841

VIRGINIA

Alexandria Mental Health
  Association
101 North Columbus Street
ALEXANDRIA, VIRGINIA
  22302
Phone: (703) 548-3810

Suicide-Crisis Center, Inc.
3636 High Street
PORTSMOUTH, VIRGINIA
Phone: (804) 399-6393

WASHINGTON

Crisis Clinic
3423 Sixth Street
BREMERTON,
  WASHINGTON 98310
Phone: (206) 373-2402

Emotional Crisis Center
1801 East Fourth
OLYMPIA, WASHINGTON
  98501
Phone: (206) 357-3681

Crisis Clinic, Inc.
1530 Eastlake East, Suite 301
SEATTLE, WASHINGTON
  98102
Phone: (206) 325-5550
       (206) 447-3210

Crisis Services
Community Mental Health
  Center
107 Division Street South
SPOKANE, WASHINGTON
  99202
Phone: (509) 838-4428/4429
  /4420

WEST VIRGINIA

Suicide Prevention Service
418 Morrison Building
815 Quarrier Street
CHARLESTON, WEST
  VIRGINIA 25301
Phone: (304) 346-3332

Contact
520 Eleventh Street
HUNTINGTON, WEST
  VIRGINIA 25705
Phone: (304) 523-3448

WISCONSIN

Walworth County Mental
  Health Center
P.O. Box 290
ELKHORN, WISCONSIN
  53121
Phone: (414) 245-5011

Emergency Services—Dane
  County Mental Health
  Center
31 South Henry Street
MADISON, WISCONSIN
  53703
Phone: (608) 251-2345

Psychiatric Emergency
   Services
Milwaukee County Mental
   Health Center
3700 West Wisconsin
   Avenue
MILWAUKEE,
   WISCONSIN 53226
Phone: (414) 257-7222

WYOMING

Help Line, Inc.
CHEYENNE, WYOMING
   82001
Phone: (307) 634-4469

Source: American Association of Suicidology

Note: In addition to the centers listed here, various churches sponsor crisis intervention centers in cities throughout the United States. These centers are listed under the name CONTACT in local telephone books. For a list of all CONTACT centers, write to: CONTACT Teleministries USA, Inc., 900 South Arlington Avenue, Room 125, Harrisburg, Pennsylvania 17109.

Bibliography

Books to Read

Alvarez, A. *The Savage God.* New York: Random House, 1972. Account of Sylvia Plath's suicide, and investigation into motives for suicide, especially among artists and writers.

Asinof, Eliot. *Craig and Joan.* New York: Viking Press, 1971. True story of two New Jersey teenagers who killed themselves in 1969 to protest Vietnam war.

Durkheim, Émile. *Suicide.* Glencoe, Illinois: The Free Press, 1951. First scientific study of suicide, originally published in French in 1897.

Friedman, Myra. *Buried Alive: The Biography of Janis Joplin.* New York: William Morrow, 1973. Powerful biography of famous rock singer who died of a heroin overdose.

Goethe, Johann Wolfgang von. *The Sorrows of Young Werther.* New York: Random House, Vintage Books, 1971. Published in 1774, this romantic novel about a young man who commits suicide had a strong influence on young people of the time.

Hendin, Herbert. *The Age of Sensation.* New York: W. W. Norton, 1975. Psychoanalytic investigation into the problems of young people today, based on studies of college students.

Howland, Bette. *W-3*. New York: Viking Press, 1974. Woman's experiences on a psychiatric ward after attempting suicide.

Lifton, Robert J. *Death in Life: Survivors of Hiroshima*. New York: Random House, 1967. Interpretation of effect of the atom bomb blast on those who survived and of attitudes of survivors of all deaths.

Menninger, Karl. *Man Against Himself*. New York: Harcourt, Brace and Company, 1938. Description and interpretation of the many self-destructive acts in which people engage.

Saint-Exupéry, Antoine de. *The Little Prince*. New York: Harcourt Brace and World, 1943. Children's classic, with strong suicidal overtones, written a year before author-aviator disappeared mysteriously on a flying mission.

Sexton, Anne. *Live or Die*. Boston: Houghton Mifflin, 1966. Includes poem "Wanting to Die," describing poet's death wishes.

Shneidman, Edwin S., ed. *Death and the College Student*. New York: Behavioral Publications, 1972. Essays about death and suicide by Harvard University students.

Vonnegut, Mark. *The Eden Express*. New York: Praeger, 1975. Son of author Kurt Vonnegut, Jr., describes his battle with schizophrenia.

Wechsler, James A. *In a Darkness*. New York: W. W. Norton, 1972. About years of mental illness and suicide of his son Michael.

More Technical Sources

Allen, Nancy, *Suicide in California, 1960–1970*. California: State Department of Health, 1974.

Ansel, Edward and McGee, Richard. "Attitudes Toward Suicide Attempters." *Bulletin of Suicidology* 8:27, Fall, 1971.

Anthony, James E. "Two Contrasting Types of Adolescent

Depression and Their Treatment." *Journal of the American Psychoanalytic Association* 18:841–859, 1970.

Balser, Benjamin and Masterson, James F. "Suicide in Adolescents." *American Journal of Psychiatry* 116:400–404, 1959.

Beck, Aaron T. *Depression.* Philadelphia: University of Pennsylvania Press, 1970.

Binswanger, Ludwig. "The Case of Ellen West." In *Existence,* edited by Rollo May, pp. 237–364. New York: Basic Books, 1958.

Blos, Peter. *On Adolescence.* Glencoe, Illinois: The Free Press, 1962.

Bronfenbrenner, Urie. "Origins of Alienation." *Scientific American* 231:53–57, August, 1974 and "Letters to the Editor" pp. 9–11, December, 1974.

Bruch, Hilde. *Eating Disorders.* New York: Basic Books, 1973.

Cain, Albert C. *Survivors of Suicide.* Springfield, Illinois: Charles C Thomas, 1972.

Cantor, Pamela. "The Effects of Youthful Suicide on the Family." *Psychiatric Opinion* 12 no. 6:6–11, 1975.

Choron, Jacques. *Suicide.* New York: Charles Scribner's Sons, 1972.

Danto, Bruce. "Assessment of the Suicidal Person in the Telephone Interview." *Bulletin of Suicidology* 8:48–56, Fall, 1971.

Dizmang, Larry H. "Loss, Bereavement and Depression in Childhood." In *Aspects of Depression,* edited by Edwin S. Shneidman and Magno J. Ortega, pp. 175–195. Boston: Little, Brown, 1969.

Dorpat, Theodore and Jackson, Joan K. "Broken Homes and Attempted and Completed Suicide." *Archives of General Psychiatry* 12:213–216, 1965.

Dublin, Louis I. *Suicide: A Sociological and Statistical Study.* New York: Ronald Press, 1963.

Erikson, Erik H. *Childhood and Society.* New York: W. W. Norton, 1963.

———. *Youth: Change and Challenge.* New York: Basic Books, 1963.

179

Farberow, Norman L. and Shneidman, Edwin S. *The Cry for Help*. New York: McGraw-Hill, 1961.

Farnsworth, Dana L. "The Young Adult: An Overview." *American Journal of Psychiatry* 131:845–851, 1974.

Finch, Stuart M. and Poznanski, Elva O. *Adolescent Suicide*. Springfield, Illinois: Charles C Thomas, 1971.

Freud, Sigmund. *Civilization and Its Discontents*. Translated and edited by James Strachey. New York: W. W. Norton, 1962.

————. "Mourning and Melancholia." In *Collected Papers*. Vol. 4, pp. 152–170. London: Hogarth Press, 1949.

Furman, Erna. *A Child's Parent Dies*. New Haven: Yale University Press, 1974.

Gould, Robert E. "Suicide Problems in Children and Adolescents." *American Journal of Psychotherapy* 19:228–246, 1965.

Grollman, Earl. *Suicide: Prevention, Intervention, Postvention*. Boston: Beacon Press, 1971.

Grunebaum, Henry V. and Klerman, Gerald L. "Wrist Slashing." *American Journal of Psychiatry* 124:527–534, 1967.

Haim, André. *Adolescent Suicide*. Translated by A. M. Sheridan Smith. New York: International Universities Press, 1970.

Hendin, Herbert. *Black Suicide*. New York: Basic Books, 1969.

————. *Suicide and Scandinavia*. New York: Grune & Stratton, 1964.

Herzog, Alfred and Resnick, H. L. P. "A Clinical Study of Parental Response to Adolescent Death by Suicide." *British Journal of Social Psychiatry* 3 no. 3:144–152, 1969.

Howells, John G. *Modern Perspectives in Adolescent Psychiatry*. New York: Brunner/Mazel, 1971.

Iga, Mamoru. "Japanese Adolescent Suicide and Social Structure." In *Essays in Self-Destruction*, edited by Edwin S. Shneidman, pp. 224–249. New York: Science House, 1967.

Jacobs, Jerry. *Adolescent Suicide*. New York: John Wiley & Sons, 1971.

Jacobziner, Harold. "Attempted Suicide in Adolescence." *Journal of the American Medical Association* 191:7–11, 1965.

Kastenbaum, Robert. "Time and Death in Adolescence." In *The Meaning of Death,* edited by Herman Feifel. New York: McGraw-Hill, 1959.

Keniston, Kenneth. *Young Radicals: Notes on Committed Youth.* New York: Harcourt Brace Jovanovich, Harvest Books, 1968.

Kiev, Ari. "Prognostic Factors in Attempted Suicide." *American Journal of Psychiatry* 131:987–990, 1974.

Lesse, Stanley, ed. *Masked Depression.* New York: Jason Aronson, 1974.

Lester, Gene and Lester, David. *Suicide: The Gamble with Death.* New York: Prentice-Hall, 1971.

Litman, Robert E. "Sigmund Freud on Suicide." In *Essays in Self-Destruction,* edited by Edwin S. Shneidman, pp. 324–344. New York: Science House, 1967.

Maguire, Daniel C. *Death by Choice.* New York: Doubleday, 1973.

Martinetti, Ronald. *The James Dean Story.* New York: Pinnacle Books, 1975.

Meeks, John E. *The Fragile Alliance.* New York: Robert E. Kreiger, 1975.

Meerloo, Joost A. M. *Suicide and Mass Suicide.* New York: Grune & Stratton, 1962.

Meyer, Bernard C. "The Little Prince: Speculation on the Disappearance of Antoine de Saint-Exupéry." *Journal of the American Psychoanalytic Association* 22:142–159, 1974.

Motto, Jerome A. and others, eds. *Standards for Suicide Prevention and Crisis Centers.* New York: Behavioral Publications, 1974.

Murphy, George E. "Suicide and the Right to Die." *American Journal of Psychiatry* 130:472–473, 1973.

Ogilvie, Daniel M., Stone, Philip J. and Shneidman, Edwin S., "Some Characteristics of Genuine vs. Simulated Suicide Notes." *Bulletin of Suicidology* 27–32, March, 1969.

Pokorny, Alex D. "A Follow-up Study of 618 Suicidal

Patients." *American Journal of Psychiatry* 122:1109–1116, 1966.

Resnick, H. L. P. "Psychological Resynthesis: A Clinical Approach to the Survivors of a Death by Suicide." In *Aspects of Depression*, edited by Edwin S. Shneidman and Magno J. Orteia, pp. 213–224. Boston: Little, Brown, 1969.

Rosenbaum, Milton and Richman, Joseph. "Suicide: The Role of Hostility and Death Wishes from the Families and Significant Others." *American Journal of Psychiatry* 126:1652–1655, 1970.

Ross, Charlotte P. "The Relationship of Crisis Intervention to Suicide Prevention." Paper delivered at the International Association for Suicide Prevention conference, Jerusalem, October, 1975.

Ross, Mathew. "Suicide Among College Students." *American Journal of Psychiatry* 126:220–225, 1969.

Schrut, Albert. "Suicidal Adolescents and Children. *Journal of the American Medical Association* 188:1103–1107, 1964.

Schrut, Albert and Michels, T. "Adolescent Girls Who Attempt Suicide." *American Journal of Psychotherapy* 23:243–251, 1969.

Schuyler, Dean. *The Depressive Spectrum.* New York: Jason Aronson, 1974.

———. "When Was the Last Time You Took a Suicidal Child to Lunch?" *Journal of School Health* 43:504–509, 1973.

Seiden, Richard H. "Campus Tragedy: A Study of Student Suicide." *Journal of Abnormal Psychology* 71:389–399, 1966.

———. *Suicide Among Youth.* U.S. Government Printing Office, Public Health Service, Publication No. 1971, Chevy Chase, Maryland: 1969.

———. "We're Driving Young Blacks to Suicide." *Psychology Today* 4:24–28, August, 1970.

Shneidman, Edwin S. *Deaths of Man.* New York: Quadrangle/The New York Times Book Company, 1973.

———. *Suicidology: Contemporary Developments.* New York: Grune & Stratton, 1976.

182

————, ed. *Essays in Self-Destruction*. New York: Science House, 1967.

————. "Suicide, Lethality and the Psychological Autopsy." In *Aspects of Depression,* edited by Edwin S. Shneidman and Magno J. Ortega, pp. 225–249, Boston: Little, Brown, 1969.

————. "Suicide: A Taboo Topic." In *Taboo Topics,* edited by Norman L. Farberow. New York: Atherton Press, 1963.

Shneidman, Edwin S. and Farberow, Norman L., eds. *Clues to Suicide*. New York: McGraw-Hill, 1957.

Shneidman, Edwin S. and Mandelkorn, Philip. "How to Prevent Suicide," Public Affairs Pamphlet No. 406. Washington: Public Affairs Pamphlets, Inc., 1967.

Shneidman, Edwin S., Farberow, Norman L. and Litman, Robert E., eds. *The Psychology of Suicide*. New York: Science House, 1970.

Stengel, Erwin. *Suicide and Attempted Suicide*. Baltimore: Penguin Books, 1970.

Stone, Michael H. "The Parental Factor in Adolescent Suicide." *International Journal of Child Psychotherapy* 2:163–201, 1973.

Tabachnick, Norman. "The Psychology of Fatal Accident." In *Essays in Self-Destruction,* edited by Edwin S. Shneidman, pp. 399–413. New York: Science House, 1967.

Teicher, Joseph D. and Jacobs, Jerry. "Adolescents Who Attempt Suicide." *American Journal of Psychiatry* 122:1248–1257, 1966.

Toolan, James M. "Depression in Childre nand Adolescents." *American ournal of Orthopsychiatry* 32:405–415, 1962.

————. "Suicide and Suicidal Attempts in Children and Adolescents." *American Journal of Psychiatry* 118:719–724, 1962.

Treffert, Darold A. "Why Amy Didn't Live Happily Ever After." *Prism,* November, 1974.

Wallace, Samuel E. *After Suicide*. New York: John Wiley & Sons, 1973.

Weiner, Irving B. *Psychological Disturbances in Adolescence.* John Wiley & Sons, 1970.

Weissman, Myrna M. "The Epidemiology of Suicide Attempts, 1960–1971." *Archives of General Psychiatry* 30:737–745, 1974.

West, Donald J. *Murder Followed by Suicide.* Cambridge: Harvard University Press, 1966.

World Health Organization. *Prevention of Suicide.* Public Health Papers No. 35. Geneva, 1968.

————. *Suicide and Attempted Suicide.* World Health Papers No. 58, Geneva, 1974.

Zilboorg, Gregory. "Differential Diagnostic Types of Suicide." *Archives of General Psychiatry* 35:270–291, 1936.

Index

187